Best walks in Southern Wales

Best Walks in Southern Wales

Richard Sale

REVISED EDITION

Frances Lincoln

Frances Lincoln Ltd
4 Torriano Mews
Torriano Avenue
London NW5 2RZ
www.franceslincoln.com

This revised edition published by Frances Lincoln 2006
First published in Great Britain 1990 by Constable and Company Ltd
Copyright © Frances Lincoln 2006
Original text © Richard Sale 1990
Preface to the revised edition and revisions to text © Richard Sale 2006
Photographs on pages 103, 107, 146 and 173 © Nathan Sale 2006; all others
    © Richard Sale 2006
Revised edition designed by Kevin Brown at park44.com

With the agreement of the Ordnance Survey the sketch maps in this book are
based on out of copyright maps amended by eye and GPS, and with additional
features – walls, fences, gates, stiles etc – added.

British Library Cataloguing in Publication data
A catalogue record for this book is available from the British Library.

Printed and bound in Singapore

ISBN 0711 2 2486 2

9 8 7 6 5 4 3 2 1

frontispiece: The Preseli Hills, looking west from Foel Drygarn

Contents

Preface to the Revised Edition

In the years since the first publication of this collection of walks in southern Wales changes have occurred on some of the routes. Many of these changes have been minor – a new gate or stile here and there, perhaps a little re-routing – but there have been instances where the changes have been more major. To ensure, as far as possible, that the walks are up to date they have been rewalked, the route descriptions and maps amended. The Forest of Dean walks required more radical surgery, changes having so altered the walking landscape that one old route has disappeared. That route has been replaced, while another has needed drastic re-alignment. But in each case the essence of the local area of the forest has been maintained. With these changes included, the collection still includes the Best Walks in southern Wales.

I thank all those with whom I have shared walks in southern Wales, but most particularly Mike Rogers. I thank my wife for her help with both the walking and the preparation of the book. I also thank Nathan Sale for allowing the use of some of his photographs.

Richard Sale, January 2006

Introduction

This companion volume to *Best Walks in North Wales* uses the same selection criteria as were applied for that volume. The three dozen routes have therefore been selected to explore the variation of scenery that southern Wales has to offer, from sea cliff, through wooded river valley and forest, to bare mountain, and to include some of the most attractive features on offer, from waterfall to mountain lake.

The routes do not concentrate on the mountains of the Brecon Beacons National Park, the area's most distinctive large scale feature, although walks within the Park form a high proportion of the routes, nor do they seek out 'unspoilt' countryside. Rather they explore the history of man in the area, from earliest times to the Celts, those folk whose name is now synonymous with Welsh history, from the Welsh princes to the industries that exploited the mineral wealth of the Principality.

Most of the routes are circular. Exceptions exist only where to have 'bent' a route would have affected its character. In these (very few) cases suggestions on transport are made.

Finally, while every effort has been made to produce comprehensive and intelligible descriptions, and to back these up with equally clear maps, it must be emphasised that these should not be seen as anything but a supplement to possession of the maps mentioned at the start of each walk. Should you go off route, for whatever reason, only possession of the correct map will assist you back on to the correct line, or back to your transport.

STRUCTURE OF BOOK

Because the area covered by the book is a large one, the walks have not been grouped together by category (see below for a def-inition of the walk categories), but by area or hill range. To help with a choice of route in the appropriate category, all the walks are given at the end of this section in increasing order of difficulty, i.e. the easiest first, the most difficult last.

Each of the areas or hill ranges is dealt with in a separate chapter, and the introduction to each chapter deals briefly with the partic-ular historical, geography aspects of the area. In addition there is a section (see 'Setting the Scene') that deals with the history of Wales, and southern Wales in particular, which will help relate a walk to the history of a particular area.

The walks have been divided into three categories, Easy, Inter-mediate and Difficult, the divisions making allowances not only for the time that a walk takes, but also for the terrain it crosses, and for the amount, and severity, of any climbing it involves. In broad terms, an Easy walk will take about two hours, an Intermediate walk up to twice as long, a good half-day's outing, while a Difficult walk will take more than about four hours and will, for most peo-ple, be a long half-day's, or day's outing. As will be seen from the table of walks at the end of this section there are also a handful of walks that lie on the border between the categories. Those that lie between Easy and Intermediate are walks that cover easy ground, but take rather longer than other Easy walks without really war-ranting the higher classification. Those that lie between Inter-mediate and Difficult cover rough ground with few landmarks, but are, relatively, short and flat.

The time given to each walk has been calculated using Naismith's Formula, a well-known walking aid, which allows one hour for each 5 map-kilometres (3 map-miles) covered by an unladened walker, and adds half an hour for each 300m (1000ft) of ascent. For most people this formula will *under-estimate* the time taken on a walk, and the under-estimation will increase as the time given for a walk increases. The reasons for this are several: firstly, no one will complete a walk in route-march style, but will pause occasionally to admire the view or watch the wildlife, and no allowance for these stops has been made; secondly, the formula makes no allowance for the roughness or otherwise of the terrain or for the effects of the weather; thirdly, no allowance has been made for rest stops, and these may be both more frequent and longer on the longer walks; and finally, the formula assumes that the walker can maintain his level of performance indefinitely. While some people can maintain 'Naismith' walking for many hours at a stretch, many, especially those new to mountain walking, tire quickly and find not only that their rest stops increase and become longer but that they cover less ground while they are actually moving.

It is imperative, therefore, that the reader should use the walk-times as a guide only, and that newcomers to the area or to the sport should attempt lower-graded walks initially, and compare their actual performance with the given walk-time in order to gauge how long the more difficult walks will take them.

THE WALKS

Name/Area/Number	Length in kms	Ascent in metres	Time in hours	Terrain and special difficulties
EASY				
Cwmystwyth Elenydd (5b)	2½	Flat	½	Paths.
The Afon Ystwyth Elenydd (5a)	1½	60	½	Grass, occasionally boggy.
Blaenafon The Valleys (32)	4	40	1	Roads.
Dinas Elenydd (8)	3½	60	1	Paths, some very stony and uneven.
Castlemartin Pembrokeshire (12a)	6	Flat	1¼	Paths (within a danger area).
The Hyddgen Valley Plynlimon (2)	6	50	1½	Paths, stony.

Name/Area/Number	Length in kms	Ascent in metres	Time in hours	Terrain and special difficulties
The Monmouthshire and Brecon Canal Abergavenny (31)	7	60	1¾	Paths.
The Cothi Valley Elenydd (7)	6	60	1¾	Roads and indistinct paths on grass.
Llyn y Fan Fach Mynydd Ddu (16a)	5	250	1¾	Path.
Bosherston Lily Ponds Perbrokeshire (12b)	8	60	2	Paths and road.
Skirrid Mountain Abergavenny (30)	6	300	2	Paths, some steep.
Water-Break-Its-Neck Radnor Forest (9)	3	40	1	Track and board-walks.
Mynydd Troed Black Mountains (25)	8	350	2½	Paths and grass.
Boughrood The Wye Valley and the Forest of Dean (33)	10	30	2½	Road and paths.
EASY/INTERMEDIATE				
Symonds Yat The Wye Valley and the Forest of Dean (34)	8	20	2½	Paths, some steep.
The Teifi Pools Elenydd (6)	7	50	2	Paths and rough grass, occasionally boggy.
Carreg Cennen Mynydd Ddu (14)	8	2500	2½	Paths, some indistinct.
INTERMEDIATE				
Caves and Waterfalls Forest Fawr (18)	8	150	2	Paths, some stony others very steep.
Penrhiw-Wen Elenydd (4)	11	150	3	Paths and pathless rough grass.
Owain Glyndwr's Way Plynlimon (3)	13	300	3½	Paths and pathless grass, some steep slopes

Name/Area/Number	Length in kms	Ascent in metres	Time in hours	Terrain and special difficulties
Rhossili, Gower (13)	9	200	3½	Paths, some at cliff edge. Very rough if the crossing to Worm's Head is made. (including Worm's Head)
St David's Pembrokeshire (10)	15	90	3½	Paths.
The Grwyne Fawr Valley Black Mountains (28)	12	500	4½	Paths and tracks.
INTERMEDIATE/DIFFICULT				
The Heart of the Forest (35)	14	250	3½	Paths and tracks.
The Llangattock Quarries Llangattock Escarpment (24)	10	200	2½	Paths and rough moor.
Chartists' Cave Llangattock Escarpment (23)	11	250	3	Rough moor.
Tommy Jones Memorial Walk Brecon Beacons (19)	9½	500	3¾	Paths.
DIFFICULT				
The Preseli Hills Pembrokeshire (11)	16	350	4	Paths, some indistinct. (Information for one-way tranverse).
Bryn Teg Brecon Beacons (21)	14	650	4½	Paths.
Llyn y Fan Fach Mynydd Ddu (16b)	10	700	4	Path, some indistinct or non-existent.
Llanthony Priory Black Mountains (29)	16	750	4½	Paths and tracks.
The Horns of Mynydd Ddu Mynydd Ddu (17)	14	750	4½	Paths, sometimes indistinct or non-existent, over rough moor.

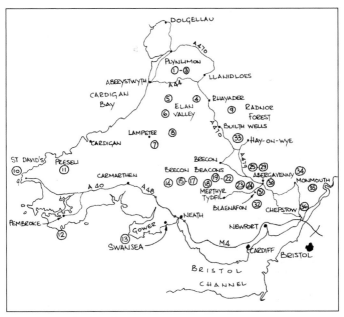

Starting points for the walks

Name/Area/Number	Length in kms	Ascent in metres	Time in hours	Terrain and special difficulties
The Eastern Beacons Brecon Beacons (22)	12	550	4½	Paths.
The Neuadd Reservoirs Brecon Beacons (20)	16	750	5	Paths.
Waun Fach Black Mountains (26)	16	750	5	Paths and rough moor.
Table Mountain Black Mountains (27)	18	680	5	Paths.
Pen Pumlumon Fawr Plynlimon (1)	10	400	3½	Paths, some indistinct. Some rough ground.

Name/Area/Number	Length in kms	Ascent in metres	Time in hours	Terrain and special difficulties
Deepest Mynydd Ddu Mynydd Ddu (15)	14	500	4	Paths, sometimes indistinct or non-existent, over barren moor. (Information for one-way traverse).
Lower Wye The Wye Valley and the Forest of Dean (36)	20	500	5	Paths, some steep.

THE WELSH LANGUAGE

The Celtic language that crossed to Britain from continental Europe split into two variants, the Goidelic language occurring in Ireland, Scotland and the Isle of Man, the Brythonic language in Wales and Cornwall. The two variants are now differentiated as 'Q Celtic' – Goidelic Celtic or Gaelic – and 'P Celtic' – Welsh, Cornish and the similar language of Brittany, Breton. The reason for the definition is in the pronunciation of 'qu'. Q Celtic pronounces this as 'c', while P Celtic pronounces it as 'p'. An easy illustration is the difference in the word for mountain. Welsh has *pen*, while Gaelic has *ceann*.

To the English eye the Welsh language is an unreadable mass of vowel-less words, consonants back-to-back. This impression is based on the misconception that the alphabets of the two languages are the same. In fact Welsh has extra consonants, 'dd', 'll' and 'ff' being letters – not as strange as it seems, for remember that English has 'w', i.e. 'uu' – and can utilise 'w' and 'y' as vowels. While 'dd' and 'll' have their own sounds – the former as 'th'; the latter as 'thl' – 'ff' is pronounced 'f', the Welsh 'f' being pronounced 'v'. Thus Tryfan is pronounced 'Tryvaen' and cwm (a corrie or mountain hollow) is pronounced 'coom'. A second, and radical, departure from English is initial mutation, the alteration of the initial consonants of words when the final sound of the preceding word is of particular form. The reason for this appears to be straightforwardly aesthetic. However the (apparently random) interchangeability of, say, *fawr* and *mawr* (large) or *fach* and *bach* (small), not to mention other worse forms, e.g. *cam – gam – ngham – cham*, makes the casual observer wince.

Throughout the book the common form of place-names has been used, even when this has meant using an English version rather than the orthodox Welsh. Thus, for instance, the eastern range of hills in the Brecon Beacons National Park has been called Mynydd Ddu rather than Black Mountain (no final 's') or Carmarthen Van, while the western arm has been called the Black Mountains (with a final 's').

An attempt at a comprehensive glossary of useful Welsh words is obviously doomed to failure, but the following is, hopefully, a useful short list, to allow the walker to better understand the ground being traversed.

Aber, confluence, but usually a river mouth
Afon, river
Allt (*Gallt*), hill, especially if wooded
Bach (*Fach*, *Bychan*), small
Bedd, grave
Betws, Chapel
Blaen, head of valley
Bont, bridge
Braich, arm
Bwlch, pass
Cadair, chair
Caer, fort
Capel, chapel
Carn (*Carnedd*), a pile of stones
Carreg, stone

Castell, castle
Cau, deep hollow
Cefn, ridge
Clogwyn, cliff
Coch (*Goch*), red
Coed, wood
Craig, crag
Crib, comb, narrow ridge
Cwm, mountain hollow, a valley with a backslope, as in the famous usage in Western Cwm below Everest
Dinas, town or hill-fort
Du (*Ddu*), balck
Dwr, water
Dyffryn, valley
Eglwys, church

Eira, Snow
Esgair, long ridge
Ffordd, road, pathway
Ffynnon, well, spring
Glas (*Las*), blue-green
Gribin, jagged ridge
Gwyn, white
Gwynt, wind
Hafod, summer dwelling, hillside house for summer use
Hen, old
Hendre, winter dwelling, valley house for winter use
Hir, long
Isaf, lowest
Llech, flat stone
Llethr, slope
Llithrig, slippery
Llyn, lake
Maen, stone (*maen hir*, long stone or standing stone, i.e. menhir)
Mawr (*Fawr*), big
Moel (*Foel*), bare, rounded hill

Mynydd (*Fynydd*), mountain
Nant, stream, brook
Newydd, new
Ogof, cave
Pant, small hollow
Pen, peak
Pistyll, waterfall, usually a water spout
Pont (*Bont*) bridge
Porth, gate
Pwll, pool
Rhaeadr, waterfall
Rhyd, ford
Saeth, arrow
Sarn, causeway
Sych, dry
Tref, town
Twll, hole
Ty, house
Uchaf, highest
Waun, moor
Wen, white
Y(*Yr*), the, of the
Ynys, island
Ysgol, ladder

MOUNTAIN SAFETY AND THE COUNTRY CODE

In comparison with the mountains of North Wales where the closeness of the Irish Sea increases the rate of fall of temperature with altitude and also enhances local winds, the hill ranges of South Wales, i.e. of the Brecon Beacons National Park, appear benign. True there is the same chilling effect with altitude, but it is less pronounce – about 1°C/150 metres (20°F/500ft) – and the change in altitude is less. Nevertheless, to a wet, cold and lost walker these hills are real enough and the walker must be prepared for harsh conditions, particularly if he is on the hills in winter.

These comments are not made to make the hills seem a playground for supermen, or to dissuade anyone from walking on them. It is just that it would be irresponsible not to warn any newcomer to mountain areas of the tricks they can play. Be prepared: if you have not done so already, get a copy of *Safety on Mountains*, a small booklet (or video) from the British Mountaineering Council (BMC) that tackles the very large subject of individual responsibility and safety. The BMC also publishes other useful booklets, including the *Hillwalking Handbook*.

It is also important that anyone contemplating expeditions into mountainous areas should be able to use a map and compass, even if they are familiar with the use of a GPS system. Again BMC publications are available to help newcomers to develop their skills, with booklets such as *Mountain Navigation* and *Navigation for Walkers*.

The majority of the walks in the book follow distinct paths. Please keep to them. The major pollution problem in the National Parks is people, and the cars that bring them. Under the sort of traffic some of the hills receive the laid pavements in towns would groan after a few months. So, if on any of the walks the path is diverted to allow the ground to recover, or if there is a section of constructed pathway, be sympathetic to the problems. Of course it would be better if there were no obvious, scarring paths, but the only really successful method of reducing wear to zero would be ban all walkers.

The Country Code

The Original Code was prepared by the Countryside Commission many years ago and remains a sensible set of 'rules' for the walker. The Code was:

Enjoy the country and respect its life and work.
Guard against all risk of fire.
Fasten all gates.
Keep dogs under close control.
Keep to public footpaths across all farmland.
Use gates and stiles to cross field boundaries.
Leave all livestock, machinery and crops alone.
Take your litter home.
Help to keep all water clean.
Protect wildlife, plants and trees.
Make no unnecessary noise.

However, in recent times the publishing organisation has become the Countryside Agency and following the enactment of 'right to roam' legislation the code has become the Countryside Code, with sections applicable to both the public and land managers:

For the Public
Be safe – plan ahead and follow any signs.
Leave gates and property as you found them.
Protect plants and animals, and take your litter home.
Keep dogs under close control.
Consider other people.

For Land Managers
Know your rights, responsibilities and liabilities.
Make it easy for visitors to act responsibly.
Identify possible threats to visitors' safety.

Setting the Scene

About 4km (2½ miles) south-east from the Gower headland overlooking Worm's Head, near Rhossili and Walk 13 of this book, is a cave in the limestone cliff, reachable only at low tide. The cave, known as Paviland Cave, was investigated in the first quarter of the 19th century by William Buckland, Oxford geologist and Dean of Westminster. He found a collection of animal bones – hyena, cave bear, woolly rhinoceros, mammoth – together with some primitive stone tools, some ivory rods and rings, pierced shells and the headless skeleton of a human being stained red by ochre. As a creationist the good Dean was much exercised by his find: here was a recognisable human sharing a cave site with animals that pre-dated Archbishop Usher's creation date of the evening of 22 October 4004 BC. The perplexed Dean decided – though whether he decided with the full vigour of intellectual honesty will never be known – that the burial was a later, Romano-British, addition to the cave. Since the skeleton was tiny he concluded it was that of a women, the Red Lady of Paviland.

Now we know that the skeleton was of a Palaeolithic, Old Stone Age, man: when he lived, perhaps 20,000 years ago, the cave would have been further from the sea, the water level having risen several feet. Why the man was headless, and why the bones had been stained with ochre, is not known, though it is speculated that there was a ritual reason, similar burials having been found elsewhere in Europe.

The Red Lady is the best Palaeolithic discovery so far in Wales, though that at King Arthur's Cave, near the River Wye and Walk 34, rivals it. For the next 15,000 years, until the Palaeolithic hunters and their Mesolithic, Middle Stone age, successors were replaced by agriculturally proficient Neolithic, New Stone Age, men, there are few remains. The Neolithic people were the first to leave a tangible sign of their existence on the landscape, for these were the cromlech builders. Cromlechs – the name is actually Welsh and is the now generally accepted word for structures also called quoits or dolmens – are burial chambers. They consist of a number of upright stones supporting a large flat roofing slab. In their original form the chambers would have been earthed over to create a long barrow, but in many instances the earth has long since weathered away to leave the uprights and cap stones, gaunt and hugely impressive against the sky.

There are several fine examples of cromlechs in southern Wales. Near Cardiff, the Tinkinswood long barrow is more or less complete, its earth mound held in place by dry-stone walling virtually indistinguishable from that which would be produced by a modern waller. Also near Cardiff, the St Lythans cromlech consists of three uprights and a single cap stone. On the Gower Peninsula, Maen Ceti, or Arthur's Stone, has a 25-ton cap stone supported by nine uprights. The name Arthur's Stone derives from a legend that Arthur was one day walking near Carmarthen, when he found a stone in his shoe. Angrily snatching it out, he flung it away – to this lonely spot on Gower. In one tale, therefore, we see the Celtic love of a superhuman hero, and recognise the awe that the cromlechs held for later inhabitants of an area. Who but a giant could raise a 25-ton stone into the air?

The best cromlech in our area is, without doubt, Pentre Ifan on the northern flank of the Preseli Hills. Here a 17-ton cap stone is supported by four uprights that taper, almost to points. The effect is, therefore, of the fingers of a hand pointing upwards to support the cap. In its original form the cromlech was covered by a mound 36m (120ft) long, a mound that would have had a walled forecourt as at Tinkinswood.

The Neolithic cromlech builders were replaced by, or evolved into, Bronze Age people who buried their dead in round barrows or cairns, and are widely believed to be responsible for the erection of *menhirs* – single standing stones, the word deriving from the Welsh, *maen hir*, long stone – and stone circles. The most prolific barrow remains are to be found on the Preseli Hills, and there are a large number of single stones scattered throughout southern Wales. Stone circles are far less numerous, and those that do exist are considerably less imposing than, say, that at Avebury. One good site, Cerrig Duon, is visited on Walk 17. This absence of stone circles is especially ironic since it has now been proven that some of the stones for Stonehenge were quarried from the eastern end of the Preseli Hills, probably by the Beaker Folk, themselves a Bronze Age people. The quarry site is visited by Walk 11, the Notes for that Walk exploring in greater depth the Stonehenge connection. Walk 4 visits an impressive menhir, Maen Serth, steeped in legend.

Following the Bronze Age, Wales saw an influx of the people with whom the country is now synonymous, the Celts. That name was not used by the Iron Age folk themselves, but derives from the Roman Keltoi, a word interchangeable with Galli, for the people who lived in Gaul or France. The Romans saw these Celts as barbaric savages, forever boasting about their own and their leaders' abilities in battles, and with a priesthood – the Druids – who were pagan mumbo-jumboists and wielded a frightening power. In reality the Celts were a cultured, civilised people, if a little warlike, whose bards – the singers of praises – compensated for the lack of a written language, and whose Druid priests practised an earth-magic no better, but certainly no worse, than that of many other ancient cults. There is evidence from the magnificent hoard of sickles, razors, fittings and so on found in 1912 in Llyn Fawr in Glamorgan, which contained both bronze and iron implements, that the Celts did not annihilate their Bronze Age predecessors. Indeed if the legend of the Lady of the Lake is a folk story then the transition from one age of the next was one of painless assimilation, a triumph for the 'barbaric' Celts. The lake of the legend is visited by Walk 16, a Note to that Walk detailing the story and its potential implications.

The most tangible reminder of the Iron Age Celts is their hill forts, defensible settlements or retreats, which are dotted all over southern Britain. Maiden Castle in Dorset is undoubtedly the best British hill fort, Tre'r Ceiri on the Lleyn Peninsula is the best in Wales, but several of our Walks visit, or go close to, good sites. Walk 10 passes a promontory fort, one built on a headland and so protected on several sides by sheer cliffs, while Walk 26 visits a fort of more conventional form.

The Romans subdued the Celts in Britain with a combination of the short sword and the seductive influence of the Roman lifestyle. They were at pains to end Druidism, invading and destroying the priesthood's island sanctuary, Anglesey, a desecration that was, in part, responsible for the uprising of Boudicca. But at first the Roman advance in Wales was resisted. One notable leader was Caratacus who rallied the Silurians and Ordovices, tribes of Wales, and fought a brave and prolonged campaign. Walk 34 visits one site that has been proposed as being important in the campaign, which ended, in AD51, with the betrayal and capture of Caratacus. So well had he fought and so impressed were the Romans with his demeanour in captivity that his life was spared and he lived in honoured and prosperous exile in Rome. To assist in the holding of Wales, the Romans built many forts connected by roads to the massive legionary fortresses at *Deva*, Chester, and *Isca*, Carleon. The latter, to the north-east of Newport, is one of the finest Roman sites in Britain, a close rival being the market town of *Venta Silurium* at Caerwent a few miles to the east. Neither of these sites is on one of our Walks, but Walk 7 does visit the Roman gold mines of Dolaucothi.

Following the departure of the Romans Britain fell to the Saxons, who landed in the east and gradually pushed westward, cutting the Celts of Wales off from those of Cornwall at the battle of Dyrham in 577. Prior to that their advance had been halted, if only for a decade or so, by a mysterious Celtic leader called Arthur, a king who is now woven into the fabric of Welsh mythology.

Arthur is found in many tales from the *Mabinogion*; there are stones and other features without number named for him; lakes abound that hold Excalibur beneath their surfaces, and secret caves where he sleeps awaiting the call to return to save his people can be found in several counties. But the tales were told by a people deprived of their country, for the Saxons took Britain right up to the borders of what is now Wales. They even named the people – these were the *Wallas*, the foreigners, the name also giving us Valais in Switzerland, and Walloon in Belgium. The Celts, by contrast, referred to themselves as Cymry, fellow countrymen, and to their country as Cymru.

The Saxon invasion of Britain showed a flaw in the Celtic tribal system that not only cost them dear then, but was to do so again and again. The Celts were very good at forming small groups and fighting amongst themselves. This inter-tribal battling was 'helped' by the system of inheritance: when a chief died his lands were divided among his sons who, if they did not fight among themselves, were usually invaded by neighbours made effectively stronger by the reduction in size of the chieftainship. Even when faced by a common enemy – Saxon, Norman or English – the Welsh could never unite for long enough to gain independence. Behind Offa's Dyke, built in the late 8th century by a Saxon king of Mercia, and followed, in part, by Walk 36, the Welsh formed and reformed small kingdoms.

Rhodri Mawr is generally named the first king, or Prince, of Wales, but though he ruled the old kingdoms – now new counties or districts – of Gwynedd, Powys and Ceredegion (Cardiganshire), he did not rule Gwent, Morgannwg (Glamorgan), Dyfed or Brycheiniog (Breconshire). A later king, Hywel Dda, Hywel the Good, whose fort is visited on Walk 27, is also mentioned as a Prince of all Wales, though he, too, ruled only the larger part of the country. Gruffydd ap Llywelyn – Gruffydd, the son of Llywelyn – did unite the country, in 1041, but he soon overreached himself by trying to expand eastward across the dyke. Edward the

Confessor sent Earl Harold Godwinson, later to be king and to die at Hastings, to deal with the usurper. Gruffydd was killed and Wales subdued.

Soon there was a new enemy, the Normans who defeated the Saxons and established along the old border a group of 'buffer states' to protect England from the Welsh. These states were the Marcher lordships, 'march' here having its original meaning of boundary. The Marcher lords were allowed to take as much of Wales they felt they could hold, a right that, not surprisingly, brought them into constant conflict with the Welsh. Some parts of Wales, chiefly the mountainous backbone and the north, the Normans left largely untouched, but the more fertile, less hostile south they did take. Here they installed a colony of Flemings from Holland and Belgium. Quite why this happened is not known: some maintain that the Flemish settlements were tolerated rather than encourage, the Flemings themselves fleeing the flooding of their own lands – at that time also under Norman domination. Others see the settlements in more political or economic terms, as deliberate actions to form a buffer, or to bring much needed agricultural or mercantile skills to a backward area. Whatever the reasons, the Flemings of Pembrokeshire and Gower were to prove a disastrous group to Welsh princes, most notably at the time of the Glyndwr rebellion.

Llywelyn ap Iorwerth, known now as Llywelyn the Great, succeeded to Gwynedd in 1203 and soon added Powys and some land in South Wales to his kingdom. He took advantage of the times, for the barons of England were combining to stand up to King John, Llywelyn's father-in-law. By siding with the barons Llywelyn was able to gain significant rights for Wales in Magna Carta, and by the time of his death in 1240 the country, while not united – the Fleming colony of the south being decidedly opposed to Welsh unity – had an air of independence.

But Llywelyn's death caused the usual fragmentation, though his grandson, Llywelyn ap Gruffydd (Llywelyn the Last) fought again for unity. He was made Prince of Wales by Henry III under the terms of the Treaty of Montgomery in 1267, but Henry's successor, Edward I, was a stronger adversary. Edward reduced Llywelyn's position to that of a baron at the Treaty of Aberconwy in 1277, a move not guaranteed to win the Welshman's heart. Llywelyn rose in rebellion again in 1282 and was killed in a minor skirmish near Builth Wells. Walk 33 lies close to the place of death of the last Welsh Prince of Wales.

Following Llywelyn's death Edward I decided that never again would he be troubled by the Welsh, and he erected his 'Ring of Stone' castles to ensure they could not rebel: Conwy, to secure the river crossing into Gwynedd; Caernarfon to ensure that the mountains of Gwynedd could not be used as a barrier; Beaumaris to secure Anglesey, the Granary of Wales, and others. These castles are in North Wales, but Walk 14 does visit Carreg Cennen, an impressive castle from earlier times in the Welsh-Norman struggle.

In the wars of Edward III the Welsh fought with distinction at Crecy and Poitiers for their English king, but the Marcher lords continued to treat their Welsh subjects with contempt, over-taxing them and using them as serfs. Finally, in 1400, following yet another clash between a Norman Marcher lord and a Welsh neighbour, there was another rebellion. Owain Glyndŵr was a strange man to lead a revolt: perhaps fifty years old, a sophisticated, educated, multi-lingual man with a distinguished record in the English king's courts and army. But lead one he did, a savage ten-year rebellion that left Wales and the Welsh exhausted and starved. Walk 2 visits the scene of Glyndŵr's first victory – over the Flemings of South Wales – while Walk 3 follows a section of a footpath named for the leader. Other walks recall events in the rebellion so far-reaching was it and so long did it last. Finally the Welsh wanted peace at any price and despite savage legislation enacted against them they still fought bravely for Henry V at Agincourt. In the Wars of the Roses that followed the Welsh were split. Even after the half-Welsh Henry Tudor landed in Pembrokeshire in 1485 and wrested the crown from Richard III at Bosworth there were some Welshmen who saw not a Welsh king but a usurper.

Henry VIII unified England and Wales, a unification that gave political rights but still allowed the Welsh to be exploited by their English neighbours. When the mineral wealth of Wales became apparent it was chiefly the Welsh who did the work, the English who took the profit. Never was this truer than in the northern slate quarries: the metal mines of mid-Wales, fine examples of which are visited by Walks 3 and 5(a), were not quite rich enough for serious long-term exploitation.

In the south the minerals were coal and iron. Both are ancient industries, dating at least from the Roman occupation, but real exploitation came only a couple of hundred years ago. The Welsh ironstone band stretched from Blaenafon to Hirwaun, about 30km (18 miles), and produced good ore with up to 40 per cent of iron. The iron was extracted in charcoal-fed forges, huge areas of forest in the lower valleys being cleared to make the fuel. Since 16 tons of wood were required to produce 1 ton of iron, the industry (and forest) was only saved by the discovery of coking coal. Coal itself had been recognised as a fuel at least by Roman times. Early mining was by means of the bell-pit. A vertical shaft was sunk until the coal seam was hit and from its base men would then work outwards into the seam, producing a hand-bell-like structure. This was hard and dangerous work: coal and men had to be hand-winched up the shaft, and since there would be many pits the horizontal digging had every chance of producing an unstable, and collapsing, roof.

Later, when shafts and digs were longer, gas rather than collapse was the major hazard, and elaborate systems for drawing air into the mine were devised. Only the introduction of the Davy lamp made working really safe: as late as 1860 over a hundred men and boys were killed in an explosion in a South Wales pit. The harsh and dangerous working conditions, poor housing and even poorer living conditions developed a strong sense of community among the miners, many of whom were not Welsh but had been brought in as cheap labour from the Midlands. The mine-owners included some colourful characters – David Davies, whose statue now dominates his native village of Llandinam near Llanidloes, was down to his last half-crown after he had paid his men, and gave that to them as well. Impressed, they gave him one last shift, and discovered the Rhondda seams, or so the story goes – but most were grey men more interested in profit than social welfare. Unionism was strongly opposed: at one gathering at Merthyr the commander of the troops called to quell and disperse the 'riot' had one of his men slice a dog in half with his sword as an example to the crowd of what could happen. The displeasure over working conditions became a more general grievance over social conditions and led to the Chartist movement, dealt with in the Note to Walk 23 which visits an important site in the movement's history. It also led to the rise in popularity of Nonconfirmist churches, the famous Valley Chapels. The established Church invariably sided with the Establishment – the mine owners – the miners seeking solace in the new branches of the faith which practised a more Christian form of Christianity.

Gradually things improved and the area became one of the mainstays of British industry. As elsewhere, however, there has now been a general decline, the iron and steel works are gone, the pits closed. Nowhere is this, or the history of both industries, better shown than at Blaenafon, the contre for Walk 32. At Blaenafon the pit-head baths have not become a supermarket, as Max Boyce's lament for a lost way of life maintains, but part of a Heritage Museum.

Plynlimon

In the middle of the nineteenth century W. F. Peacock, the traveller, wrote of his trip to Plynlimon. He encountered 'bogland; uncertain sponge, with black pitchy water... dark herbage thrives and its complexion is just about as ghostly and healthless as you can imagine'. Peacock's boots had an undeniably black baptism. He was lucky, he said, to escape from a hellish prison where a man climbing alone was 'little better than a fool. He has one chance of returning in safety; he has ninety-nine chances of being seen no more in life'.

Since then – and perhaps before – Plynlimon has had a bad press. It is 'a sodden weariness'. Even Thomas Pennant, a self-confident traveller, was dissuaded from making a visit, being informed that it was an uninteresting object, the base most extensive, the top boggy and the view over a dreary and almost uninhabited country'. As a complete contrast, it is widely believed that Coleridge thought of the line 'Water, water, everywhere. Nor any drop to drink' while on Plynlimon when he and a companion were parched with thirst during a walk across it.

Both suggestions about the range are justified, but not widely justified. It is certainly true that Plynlimon has boggy sections: the extensive peat bogs near Blaenhafren can be an 'interesting' place to be after heavy rain, and much of the upland plateau shows frequent outcrops of bog moss. And, given a few days of dry weather, the mosses dry out dramatically, to the point where they scrunch under foot, and the Mother of Rivers can then be fairly discreet about where exactly her rivers are.

Plynlimon has long been considered one of the three mountains of Wales – along with Snowdon and Cadair Idris – and is indeed of the same rock. The underlying rock is Ordovician, set among the Silurian rock like a displaced section of Snowdonia. But there is none of the rugged grandeur of the Snowdon peaks, the best Plynlimon can offer being the broken cliffs above the Rheidol's source, Llyn Llygad Rheidol. Rather, the hills here resemble the green humps of the Carneddau. It is said that when the famous Alpine guide Jean Charlet came here he gaped at the hills and claimed that God had forgotten to put tops on them. This roundness, the lowness of the hills — Pen Pumlumon Fawr does not quite make 2500 ft — and its reputation, mean that Plynlimon stays quiet when the more northerly hills are groaning under the weight of travellers. That is what I mean by having a bad press: in reality Plynlimon has much to offer: spectacular views — on a good day virtually every other mountain range in Wales can be seen — fine valleys, well set lakes, and a wealth of Celtic history and folk lore.

Conventional wisdom holds that Pen Pumlumon Fawr should be climbed from the south, from Eisteddfa Gurig, but that route commits the walker to a long ascent with limited views and few other redeeming features. We go north instead, choosing an ascent line that allows views northward to Snowdonia and of the reservoir lakes of Nant-y-moch and Llyn Llygad Rheidol. As easier walk visits the lonely Hyddgen valley, scene of a desperate battle, while a third visits the even more frequently neglected eastern side of the range.

WALK 1 | Pen Pumlumon Fawr

Our first route climbs to the highest point of the Plynlimon area, climbing from the north. The route is a shorter than that from Eisteddfa Gurig, but involves about an extra 100m (330ft) of climbing. To compensate it offers ever-better outlooks including a view of a finely set mountain lake.

Walk Category: Difficult (3½ hours) | Length: 10km (6 miles) | Ascent: 400m (1300ft) | Maps: Landranger Sheet 135; Explorer Sheet 213 | Starting and finishing point: At 769 873 beside the road on the southern edge of the Nant-y-moch reservoir. This road is reached by turning right off the mountain road from Ponterwyd to Tal-y-bont just before the reservoir dam is reached

From the metalled road a rough track rises steeply towards Llyn Llygad Rheidol (see note ①). At a gate go through, then leave the track to go east and upwards towards the obvious summit. Trend leftward to the stream of Maesnant whose slight valley can be followed to below the twin knobby summits of Pumlumon Fach. From the slightly higher – the more easterly – knob there is a fine view of Llyn Llygad Rheidol (see ① Llyn Llygad Rheidol). From the knob the summit of Pumlumon Fawr can no longer be seen, but it quickly emerges again when the ridge to the south is climbed (see ② Pen Pumlumon Fawr).

Until a few years ago the plateau-ridge to the east of Plynlimon's summit was free access land and a very fine walk could be made by way of the source of the Wye (see ③ River sources), the subsidiary summit of Pen Pumlumon-Arwystli and the source of the Severn. From there a descent route going slightly north of west reached the Hengwm valley which was followed to

Nant-y-moch reservoir

join Route 2. But then a huge new fence was constructed along the ridge, a fence that descends northward and southward, cutting off access to both the ridge and the Wye source. There are no gates or stiles, though in fairness it must be said that there is also no right of way. The route to the river sources could still be followed, but the walker would be on private land.

Our legal route follows the fence eastward in order to traverse the steep cliffs above the lake, following the eastern edge of the cwm southward to a point where a descent can be made to the outflow of the lake. From there a route can be made down the right bank of the Nant-y-Llyn to reach Route 2, but that is not much of a route, with little to compensate for the poor going. It is better to follow the track back to the start, passing an interesting collection of small pools set on a rocky plateau.

① *Llyn Llygad Rheidol*

Perhaps as little as 10,000 years ago

an ice sheet covered the summit plateau of Plynlimon, the ice flowing out in all directions. Northward the

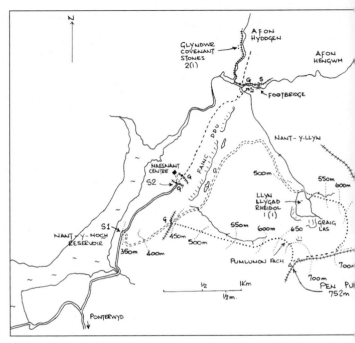

Walks 1 and 2: Plynlimon

ice scoured a hollow, over-deepening it so that when the ice melted a lake was formed behind a dam of deposited glacial moraine. Llyn Llygad Rheidol is an excellent example of such a glacially-formed lake and is beautifully set below the broken cliffs of Graig Las. Today the lake is a reservoir, as the notice with the dire threats tells the visitor, with an artificial outflow, the water directed down an ugly, but easily crossed concrete channel.

② Pen Pumlumon Fawr

The Mabinogion, *that fountain head of Celtic folklore, tells of the Arthurian knights Kay and Bedevere sitting on this summit in 'the greatest wind in the world'. Certainly the summit's position and its height — low by Snowdonian standards, but high in relation to the surrounding land — do appear to attract the wind, and there are*

SOURCE OF
RIVER SEVERN
1 (3)

600m

650m

PEN
PUMLUMON - ARWYSTLI

700m   650m   700m

650m

SOURCE OF RIVER WYE
1 (3)

FAWR

is a significant watershed and the mother of rivers – but it is certainly difficult to claim an especially noteworthy group of five.

In 1401 Owain Glyndwr raised his standard on Plynlimon, a monument near the eastern end of the Nant-y-moch dam noting the event. There followed the battle of Hyddgen, (see Note ① of Route 2). Now the Welsh for a standard is llumon, which looks suspiciously like the 'limon' of Plynlimon and the 'lumon' of Pumlumon. Is Pumlumon really Pen Llumon, the Hill of the Standard?

③ River sources

Though they are geographically close – the Wye and Severn are born about 4km (2½ miles) apart – the two river sources could hardly be more different. The Wye starts boldly, within yards it is flowing in a well-defined valley, while the Severn has no definable start, rising tentatively amid the peat bogs that make up the land between Pen Pumlumon Arwystli and Cumbiga. The names reverse the process 'Wye' is probably Celtic and probably means rapid, though little is definite. 'Severn' derives from Hafren. In Celtic legend Locrinus, the King of Britain, was married to Gwendolen,

many who have been grateful to crouch in the low-walled summit shelter. The hill's name is usually given as deriving from pump, Welsh for five, and 'an ancient word for...'. The latter is sometimes river, sometimes peak and never convincing. Certainly it is possible to distinguish five tops, but equally easy to see three or seven. The Rheidol, Wye and Severn rise here, as do many other rivers – the area

daughter of the King of Cornwall. Sadly Locrinus loved Estrildis and a daughter, Hafren, was born. Ultimately Locrinus left Gwendolen to live with Estrildis and Hafren. Outraged, Gwendolen travelled to Cornwall, raised an army and returned to wreak vengeance. Locrinus was killed in battle, and Estrildis and Hafren were bound and thrown into a nearby river. As they drowned Gwendolen realised that she should not have murdered the child as Hafren was innocent of any crime. But attempts to save the child failed and the remorseful Gwendolen named the river in her memory. In Welsh the river is still Hafren, the source being named Blaenhafren. The English form derives from the Romans, whose aspirant was 's' not 'h' and who therefore called the river Sabrina.

The land between the two rivers is known as Fferllys, and is the home of the Tylwyth Teg, the fairy folk. On this land the ferns (of which there are not many) bear a small blue flower on St John's Eve. If the seeds of the flowers are gathered in a white cloth – no hand must touch them – the gatherer will become invisible so that he/she may enter a lover's room undetected. Alternatively, if you stay in Fferllys an elf will exchange your seeds for a purse of gold.

WALK 2 | The Hyddgen Valley

This short walk visits the site of Owain Glyndŵr's first success in battle. It is a good introduction to the joys of Plynlimon.

Walk category: Easy (1½ hours) | Length: 6km (4 miles) | Ascent: 50m (150ft) | Maps: Landranger Sheet 135; Explorer Sheets 213 and 215 | Starting and finishing point: Beside the road, as for Walk 1, but closer to the road end near the farm buildings of Maesnant

---

Continue eastwards along, or beside, the road. At the road end, go through the gate to the right of the gate for Maesnant and follow the stony track beyond. To the right the steep ground of Fainc Ddu Uchaf and Fainc Ddu Isaf offers fine views. Beyond a ruin the track bears left to the River Hengwm which can be forded to reach a gate. Alternatively a path leads on past old walls to reach a footbridge. Either way the Hyddgen valley is reached, up which an indistinct path leads over peaty ground. Sadly the Cerrig Cyfamod Glyndŵr (see ① Glyndŵr Covenant Stones) are across the Afon Hyddgen and protected by a fence, but the walker can see them plainly. To return, the outward route is reversed. From the bridge a small waterfall in the Hengwm valley can be reached by following the river upstream (eastwards). The going is a little arduous however, and many will settle for the outward route with its expanding view over the Nant-y-moch reservoir.

---

① *Glyndwr Covenant Stones*

Following the Norman invasion of England the Norman kings left Wales to itself, content to place a barrier between themselves and the Welsh, their impenetrable mountains and vile weather. The barrier was human, the Marcher lords. These lords owned the land on the march,

The Hyddgen valley from near the start of the walk

or border, its eastern border being delineated, but the western boundary being undefined. In Wales they could take all the land they thought they could hold. Not surprisingly this, together with the frequent passing of anti-Welsh legislation, left Wales with a seething undercurrent of resentment. Often there were uprisings, some of them major as with the problems in the late thirteenth century that led to the building of the 'Ring of Stone' castles in north Wales.

In 1399 Henry Bolingbroke added to Welsh bitterness by usurping the crown – as many Welshmen saw it – from Richard II. Then in

1400 the new Henry IV supported Lord Grey of Ruthin against Owain Glyndŵr, a high-born Welshman whose home was at Sycharth on the flank of the Berwyns. Owain was forced to flee his comfortable home and, in revenge, led a band of men to loot the towns of Ruthin, Denbigh and Flint. To put down the incipient uprising King Henry arrived with an army: the countryside quietened and Glyndŵr disappeared. He came here, to the Hyddgen valley, where, in 1401, he was joined by a small group of men, perhaps 400 in all. News of this 'army' spread to South Wales where a group of pro-English, Flemish wool-trade settlers decided to *act swiftly to protect their interests. An armed band was formed and marched north to nip any upsurge of anti-English feeling in the bud.*

Glyndŵr was still new to rebellion and his men took none of the precautions necessary to protect themselves. Consequently the Flemish army managed to reach Plynlimon not only unmolested, but also unseen. And not only to reach Plynlimon, but to reach the ridge above the Hyddgen valley – bear in mind that in 1401 there was no Nant-y-moch reservoir. From the high ground they rushed in on Glyndŵr and his men, whom they outnumbered by perhaps as many as five to one. With retreat impossible and defeat and death probable, the Welsh fought like tigers, stemming, then turning, the Flemish flow. Against all odds Glyndŵr was victorious, the Flemish army fleeing in confusion leaving behind hundreds of dead.

News of the victory turned a local uprising into a full scale rebellion as the Welsh rallied to their new leader. Today the only sign of the battle in this peaceful valley are the two dazzling white calcite blocks that the Welsh hauled here to commemorate their victory and to pledge their support for Glyndŵr.

WALK 3 | Owain Glyndŵr's Way

This walk follows a section of Owain Glyndŵr's Way, a long-distance footpath from Knighton to Welshpool, by way of Machynlleth, originally waymarked by Powys County Council, but recently adopted as a National Trail. Owain Glyndŵr is mentioned in Note ① of Walk 2. Our route follows only a three-mile section of the fine 125-mile walk, deflecting from it to view the ruins of the mines that made Dylife, the starting village, important over a century ago.

Walk category: Intermediate (3½ hours) | Length: 13km (8 miles) | Ascent: 300m (1000ft) | Maps: Landranger Sheet 135; Explorer Sheet 215 | Starting and finishing point: At the lay-by beside the road opposite the Star Inn, Dylife. The village is reached along a narrow mountain road that leaves the B4518 just north of Staylittle and emerges at Machynlleth by way of the town golf course

From the lay-by take the signed track that rises steeply southward up the hillside. Go through a gate and leave the track, turning half-right for a gate and stile. Go through or over and follow the rutted path beyond over the summit of Penycrocbren (see ① Penycrocbren). At the summit there is another gate and stile pair beyond which the path reaches a third pair. Go through or over again and down to a track, passing yet a fourth gate and stile pair. Here Glyndŵr's Way goes right, but we go left along the track. Go through a gate and follow the track as it bends left. Technically the route goes right here, following the right of way around the hill westward. A fence has been built across the way with no stile and this necessitates a steep descent of the Afon Clywedog reached just west of the old mines (see ② Dyfngwm

The Twymyn valley below the Ffrwd Fawr waterfall

Mine). At the river a half-stile allows progress westward. The Twymyn can be followed upstream making use of a steep track which crosses a slope that is never easy and occasionally desperate. It is a most beautiful stream and enters a narrow, rocky gorge that is even more spectacular. To the right there are old water-filled shafts, the rock near them having been worked into weird shapes. There is even one keyhole through the rock.

Further progress upstream is halted by the gorge and although an escape can be made up the right side it is a steep, loose and very difficult climb. It is better to retrace, going up the steep slope to the top of the gorge as soon as possible. A definite, though sometimes indistinct, path is reached and followed leftward over a half-stile and then down to a footbridge and the Nant Goch, a tributary of the Afon Clywedog.

The bridge is not for the faint-hearted, being only two well-spaced girders for half its length and having a handrail that seems to need, rather than lend, support. Beyond, the path continues to farm buildings and a more straightforward track. Bear right where this joins another, continuing past Glaslyn (see ③ Glaslyn) to a large 'lay-by' on the left. Here we rejoin Glyndŵr's Way, but now going west-east. Go left on a grassy, rutted path and follow it to the summit of Foel Fadian (see ④ Foel Fadian). A fence of Foel Fadian's eastern flank requires a descent of the ascent path back to the track. Go left and follow the track to a minor road. Go right taking the road verge back to Dylife (see ⑤ Dylife).

① *Penycrocbren*

This hill, 466m (1530ft) high, is the 'Hill of the Gallows', so called from a supposedly legendary story told of the time when Dylife was an impor- *tant mining town. The town's only blacksmith, Siôn y Gof (John the Smith), believed that his wife was being unfaithful to him and decided to murder her. As the couple had a young daughter, Siôn knew that his*

Walk 3: Owain Glyndŵr's Way

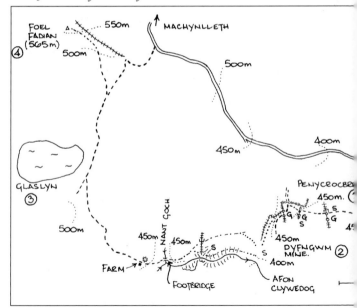

wife's lone disappearance would cause suspicions, and so he killed his daughter as well, throwing the bodies into a disused mine shaft. He told the villagers that the pair had left him, but later, by accident or by search after doubts had been raised, the bodies were found. Siôn was tried, convicted and sentenced to hang. At the time the bodies of the hanged were left to rot on gibbets as a warning, and it was decided that Siôn's body should hang in a full iron cage, his head in a smaller cage. As the only local smith Siôn was set to work to make the cage. Whether this was necessity or a calculated act of vengeance is unclear, but Siôn's last act was the construction of his own cage. He was hanged on the 'Hill of the Gallows' and gibbeted inside his own handiwork. So the legend goes.

In 1938 two men digging on the hill uncovered the cage, proving that the story was not legend but fact. Today the skull of Siôn y Gof, still in its iron cage, is displayed at the National Museum at St Fagan's near Cardiff. No civilised person can find great sympathy with a man who killed not only his wife but his own, and innocent, child, but it is difficult to view the skull without feeling a little pity for a man set such an appalling task.

Centuries before Siôn's hanging Penycrocbren – then, presumably, bearing another name – was the site of a small Roman fort, as a Roman military road traversed the northern flank of Plynlimon, on the way to Machynlleth and the Dyfi river. Today it takes an expert to discern the lines of the old walls.

② Dyfngwm Mine

The Dyfngwm Mine was only part of the Dylife mines, one of the fore-

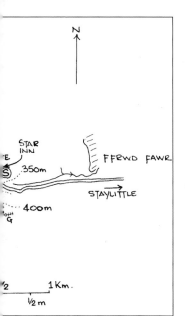

Looking north over the Dyfi Valley to Cadair Idris from Foel Fadian's summit

most mining areas of Wales. It was widely believed that it was a very rich lead mine, but its history – over a very short lifetime of around thirty years – was one of mismanagement and poor commercial sense. The mine closed in 1867, but was reopened in the early 20th century, though with little more success. The returns from the mine show that in addition to lead it produced copper and a little zinc.

The Dylife mines themselves, closer to the Star Inn, were probably worked in Roman times. Here too the ore yielded lead and copper: at the height of its prosperity the mine employed over 300 people, with the now ghostly Dylife village being a bustling place of over 1,000 inhabitants. At the site was the biggest waterwheel ever erected in Wales, the 63ft (19m) Red Wheel. Today the wheel pit is a rubbish dump.

③ Glaslyn

This fine lake is another blue-grey sheet of water bearing the name Glaslyn (blue-grey lake!). Unlike the Glaslyn that lies below Snowdon, reputed home of Excalibur and the legendary afanc, this lake is merely bottomless. Glaslyn and its surrounding area, a piece of heather moor rare on Plynlimon, are a Site of Special Scientific Interest. Ducks, swans and Goosanders winter here and the area is home of both the Peregrine Falcon and the Merlin. Equally interesting is the plant life, which includes Heath Bedstraw, Cowberry and Ivy-leaved Bellflower.

④ Foel Fadian

Foel Fadian, at 564m (1850ft), was the highest mountain in the old county of Montgomeryshire. From the summit the views are superb. To the south is Plynlimon, a shapelier block than many give it credit for, while northward are the hills of Snowdonia. Equally good is the view west, over the farmland of the southern side of the Dyfi valley, the river itself and Cardigan Bay. Foel Fadian offers what is arguably the best sunset viewpoint in this book.

⑤ Dylife

The Star Inn and the cemetery with its rusting ironwork and shattered gravestones seem to belie the fact that the village was once home to over 1,000 people – a big village locally, even by the standards of the day. The village name derives from 'flood' or 'torrent', and it is generally believed that this is a reference to Ffrwd Fawr, the 'big stream', a spectacular waterfall a kilometre or so east of the village. At 45m (150ft) Ffrwd Fawr is one of the highest free-falling waterfalls in Wales and is extraordinary for the volume of water that falls, the Afon Twymyn that feeds it rising only about 4km (2½ miles) from the head. Below the hard sandstone horseshoe of the falls the Twymyn turns sharply northward, flowing through a magnificent, almost textbook, glaciated valley.

Elenydd

South of Plynlimon is a high plateau of barren moorland deeply cut by river valleys. To the west the plateau fails to reach the shore of Cardigan Bay, falling gracefully to become the eastern side of the Teifi valley, while to the south it extends as far as Llandovery. Eastward the boundary is the valley road between Llandovery and Llandrindod Wells, the hills of Mynydd Eppynt to the east of the A483 being quite different. North of Llandrindod the situation is less clear. The plateau there actually extends to the English border, though it is usually sub-divided. To the east of Llandrindod is the Radnor Forest, while to the north of the town is a lower, more cultivated landscape that is crossed by Owain Glyndŵr's Way. West of Llandrindod, indeed west of the Wye valley that cuts decisively through the plateau, is the real Elenydd, a land of uncompromising, barren moor, deeply dissected by valleys that have been flooded to form the reservoirs of Claerwen and the Elan valley, the flooding provided drinking water for the Midlands. The facts about the dams, the surface area, volume of water, and daily flows are staggering, but it is always an emotive point when wild Welsh land is deluged to satisfy an English thirst. The loss of heritage can be severe. Here Cwm Elan was lost, a house once occupied by the poet Shelley whose eccentricities – including the sailing of boats made from five-pound notes on the local stream – no doubt kept the locals in gossip for weeks.

The name Elenydd is stolen from Giraldus Cambrensis, Gerald of Wales. This part-Norman, part-Welsh cleric was born – in the magnificent castle of Manorbier in southern Pembrokeshire, near to Walk 12 – in the mid-12th century and journeyed around Wales in 1188 with Archbishop Baldwin to gain support for the Third Crusade. Gerald was an ambitious man who wanted to be

Archbishop of St David's. He was also outspoken and blessed with a gift for invective. The latter traits were at odds with the former ambition and Gerald died in obscurity in the early part of the 13th century. He would be forgotten today, except perhaps by the persistent historian, were it not for two books that he wrote on his Welsh travels. One, *The Journey through Wales*, is a description of the Baldwin journey, the other, *The Description of Wales*, is a geographical, socio-economic study. Each is brilliant, the first having a chastening effect on all who write on travelling in Wales, being at once the first book written on the subject and (arguably) the best.

Gerald used the word Elenydd to differentiate the mountains of southern Wales from those of Eryri in North Wales. From this geography it is clear that he means the area described above, an area for which there is now no accepted name. It is widely assumed that the name derives from the Afon Elan, the flooding of whose valley yielded the Craig Goch, Penygarreg, Carreg-ddu and, in part, Caban-coch reservoirs. Tantalisingly, Gerald reveals that in 'English' the area was known as Moruge, a name that has not only become extinct, but defies explanation.

In its northern and central sections Elenydd is not a land to be trifled with, being devoid of real features and paths, with a vegetation that can make strong walkers weep and a lack of habitation that makes it feel remote and vaguely hostile. It is a place for the well-equipped and experienced walker to find peace and an inner challenge, but a difficult place to offer a walk which both does justice to the area and does not place the walker in a potentially unfriendly position.

Our first walk makes use of a couple of well-defined ridges to explore some good views and a couple of interesting ancient sites. The second walk has two variations, one a fine river valley, the other a fascinating industrial archaeological site. The third walk takes a tour around some smaller lakes, visiting the real Elenydd in a controlled way.

WALK 4 | Penrhiw-Wen

Between the Elan valley reservoirs and the Wye valley the Elenydd plateau is partially split by a tumbling stream. This walk takes the ridges that define that stream's valley, ridges which offer fine views of the Wye and Elan valleys.

Walk category: Intermediate (3 hours) | Length: 11km (7 miles) | Ascent: 150m (500ft) | Maps: Landranger Sheet 143 or 136; Explorer Sheet 200 | Starting and finishing point: Leave Rhayader south-westward on the B4518, the road to the Elan valley. Just beyond Cwmdeuddwr, about 600m from Rhayader's centre, a mountain road for Aberystwyth leaves rightwards. Take this. Beyond the forest the road climbs steadily. Park in one of the numerous pull-ins on this road, as close as possible to a point where the stream to the left runs into small pond created by a dam/sluice. Ahead and left at this point there is a large sheepfold

Almost opposite a convenient pull-in close to the pond (at 930 699) a rutted track heads uphill, eastwards. Take this and follow it up and across a rugged plateau where wheatears and whinchats are often seen. The track dips and joins another, but the first objective, the standing stone of Maen Serth, is now visible on the hill crest ahead (see ① Maen Serth). Retrace the route to the dip, then take a distinct track that heads off right to contour along the cliffs of Cerrig-gwalch. At any suitable point, but best at about half-distance along the cliff, turn south-west (that is left, then half-left again) and head across the moor to a rutted track going north-west to south-east (that is left to right). Go right along this, passing a small, robust standing stone (see ② Maengwyngweddw). Continue to the road.

Maen Serth

Cross the road and take the gentle, left-curving ridge that rises on the other side. Follow this to its top and then turn south-eastward for the obvious top of Crugyn Ci across the boggy plateau ahead. Crugyn Ci has a trig point summit, which has to be searched for among the outcrops, and is a fine viewpoint (see ③ Crugyn Ci). Now follow the direction offered by a trio of modern concrete posts that point towards a small copse. Follow that line until a vague track is reached contouring the hillside. Go left along it, and leave it at any convenient point where the steepish valley side can be descended. To the left as you descend, beyond the obvious sheepfold, are the remains of a Roman fort similar to that on Penycrocbren hill on Walk 3, and equally elusive to the amateur's eye. It is said that from the air, or when there is a light snow covering, the outline of the fort is plainly visible. Cross the stream easily, but with care, to regain the start.

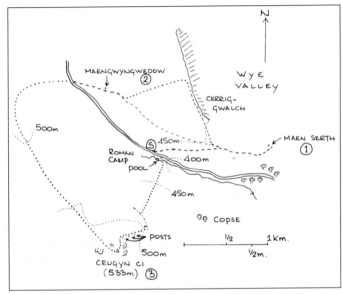

Walk 4: Penrhiw-Wen

① *Maen Serth*

Standing stones have held a fascination for man ever since their original erection, which was probably as early as the Neolithic period and was certainly the Bronze Age. Even today there is a power in such stones, particularly when, as here, they stand in isolated, romantic splendour. Maen Serth is the 'steep stone', a tall monolith that dominates the skyline for much of the early part of our walk. The slight ambiguity over the age of the mono-

lith is not helped by a find from a cairn near it and, indeed, on our route, but too damaged to be of any interest to (or even to be recognised by) the layman. At Clap-y-arian a stone axe was found, but of a design favoured by the Beaker folk, the Bronze Age builders of Stonehenge, who knew how to use metal, but had insufficient of it for their needs. Mention of Stonehenge is of interest here, as the axe was found to be of Preseli stone, perhaps from a Stonehenge bluestone quarry. The axe also suggests a cross-country trade route – what a fine walk that would be if it were rediscovered.

In the late 12th century the country around Rhayader was disputed by Roger Mortimer, the local Norman Marcher lord, and the Welsh chieftains Rhys ap Gruffydd and the brothers Cadwallon and Einion Clud. The dispute spilled over into occasional violence, but earned each man the respect of the others. Consequently at Christmas 1176 all four men gathered at Rhys's castle to feast and joust. Einion Clud defeated Roger Mortimer in the joust, the Norman lord showing his contempt for good sportsmanship by ambushing the Welshman as he returned home. Einion Clud was killed – as was his brother a little later, also by Mortimer – on this Elenydd ridge. Traditionally the killing was at Maen Serth, which is, as a consequence, also known locally as the Prince's Stone. Interestingly serth is also Welsh for obscene, a meaning which a murder site could easily assume.

After the death a cross was incised on the stone as a memorial, though it is now almost impossible to see the carving beneath the lichen cover. But there is another interpretation of the events, see Note ② below.

From Maen Serth the view across Rhayader and the country beyond is superb. In the other direction the wooded cliffs of Cerrig-gwalch are equally eye-catching, though walkers will doubtless have mixed opinions of the power-generating windmills which now top Moelfryn.

② Maengwyngweddw

This shorter less conspicuous stone stands closer to the road and below a small ridge – a much more convenient place for an ambush than the site of Maen Serth. Another version of the Einion Clud murder story outlined in Note ① above has Clud murdered here, the stone being named for his surviving wife, the Welsh name translating as the 'White Stone of the Widow'.

That leaves the problem of the incised cross on Maen Serth, but there is yet another tradition that a medieval judge was murdered there en route to, or from, the Rhayader assize, and that the cross commemorates his killing. A more prosaic explanation is that the carving was the 'Christianising' of a pagan monolith, an attempt by an awe-struck populace to reduce the power of the stone. Many examples of this are known, from the intricate carving of crosses on the tops of huge menhirs in Brittany to the church-led, annual ritual destruction of stones from the Avebury Circle which lasted until only a century or two ago.

③ Crugyn Ci

As a viewpoint Crugyn Ci suffers from a plateau-like summit that hides from the walker a view of the Elan valley reservoirs. However, the deep gash of the valley itself is visible, as is the huge expanse of rolling moorland of Elenydd. Away from the moor the Wye valley offers a fine view eastward.

WALK 5 | (a) The Afon Ystwyth and (b) Cwmystwyth

Further west along the mountain road to Aberystwyth that took us to the start of Walk 4 is some exquisite scenery and two fine short walks that explore the varied country and heritage of the northern end of Elenydd. Both take the banks of the Afon Ystwyth, but they could hardly be more dissimilar.

Walk category: (a) Easy (½ hour); (b) Easy (½ hour) | Length: (a) 1½ km (1 mile); (b) 2½ km (1½ miles) | Ascent: (a) 20m (60ft); (b) Flat | Maps: (a) and (b) Landranger Sheet 135 or 136: (a) Explorer Sheet 214; (b) Explorer Sheet 213

(A) THE AFON YSTWYTH

Westward from Maen Serth the mountain road reaches the head of the Craig Goch reservoir where the Elan valley road turns left (south) over Pont ar Elan. Continuing along the visitor is following an old turnpike road and passes, at 871 741, the ruins of Hillgate, an old toll-gate house. Hillgate was destroyed during the local Rebecca riots of 1843-4. The rioters were locals who dressed as women and blackened their faces. They took their name from the Old Testament character, and justified their activities by noting the Testament's advice that they should rise up and possess the gates of their oppressors. The rioters were protesting about the iniquities of the turnpike system which forced the locals to pay tolls for the use of roads that were never maintained and to which there was no realistic alternative.

Starting and finishing point: West again from the ruins of Hillgate there is a fine bog, Gors Lwyd, to the left. Beyond, the

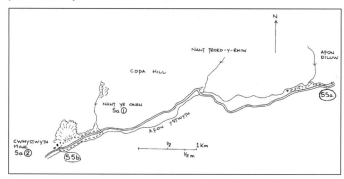

Walk 5: (a) The Afon Ystwyth and (b) Cwmystwyth

road swings leftward and reaches, at 849 757, a small pull-in to the right.

From the pull-in go down over steepish, slightly boggy ground to the stream, the fledgling Afon Ystwyth, and follow it to its confluence with the Afon Diluw. Follow the river downstream for any distance from a few hundred metres to 1km (½ mile). The river is very beautiful, with occasional water-hollowed rocks and fine plant life. The far riverside has a path that leads back up the Afon Diluw, but crossing the Afon Ystwyth is not easy unless the water level is very low.

(B) CWMYSTWYTH

West of the start of Walk 5(a) are the ruins of the Cwmystwyth mine. This is an eerie site, and also a very dangerous one for the unwary or for unrestrained children. But it is also a fascinating site, and perfectly safe if sensible precautions are observed.

Starting and finishing point: At any of a number of places near (803 745), at the western end of the mining site.

From the start go down to the river and, turning left (eastward), follow it upstream to the far end of the mine site. This is recog-

Mining ruins, Cwmystwyth

nisable from the steep gash through the rocks above the mine site that brings the Nant yr Onen stream (see ① Nant yr Onen) down to the Afon Ystwyth. The Nant forces the walker on to the road which gives access to the mine site, its huge tips, shafts, pools and rubbish. With caution the walker can visit the sites (see ② Cwmystwyth Mine), experiencing at first hand the desolation. But please beware – of all buildings, which are very unstable, of old shafts, some of which are partially filled and so look innocuous, and of the occasional unstable heap of old rubbish that has the potential to badly cut a slipping leg.

① Nant yr Onen

② Cwmystwyth Mine

The Cwmystwyth Mine produced not only lead but copper, the copper ore being chiefly found on Copper Hill, drained on its western side by the Nant yr Onen. Interestingly the hill's name is now most frequently rendered as Copa Hill, copa being Welsh for a crest. This is barely acceptable geographically and it seems more likely to be a 'Welshised' version of the English name. The hill's copper ore was exposed by hushing, a process in which artificial reservoirs were created on the hillside, the water in them being released quickly to scour away the topsoil of the hill and so reveal the ore. The hushing scars that radiate out from the Nant yr Onen are believed to be the finest remains of the technique in Britain.

In 1872 the Cwmystwyth Mine was noted as being 'both the richest and the oldest wrought mine in the county (of Cardiganshire)' and as having produced, by that time, more than two million pounds' worth of lead ore. That money came from the extraction and crushing of perhaps 100,000 tons of rock. In its early days the mine shafts for lead ore were dug horizontally into the hillside, vertical shafts only being introduced when a 30-ft waterwheel was erected to power pumps to extract water, seepage always being a local problem. By the last years of the 19th century the mine was finding it hard to compete, and it finally closed in 1921.

WALK 6 | The Teifi Pools

This route takes a narrow, no-through road that penetrates deep into Elenydd from the west, using a series of small pools to act as a guide through some lovely, but lonely countryside, reminiscent of deepest Elenydd, but more 'user-friendly'. That said, the going is a little uncompromising, turning an easy walk into one requiring a little more effort.

Walk category: Easy/Intermediate (2 hours) | Length: 7km (4½ miles) | Ascent: 50m (160ft) | Maps: Landranger Sheets 135 or 147; Explorer Sheets 213 and 187 | Starting and finishing point: Take the road that leaves the B4343 eastward at the inn in Ffair Rhos, a little north of Pontrhydfendigaid. Follow the narrow, occasionally blind-bended, road for about 4km (2½ miles). After a steep rise there is a zig-zag across a bridge. Park at a pull-in on the right, beyond the bridge, at 779 682

Follow the road – but do not walk on it, take the verge to one side or the other – among some magnificent rock scenery to a lane right that leads to Llyn Egnant, the last of the pools. The lane is obvious, but eventually peters out into an undrivable – except by four-wheel drive – moorland track. Go down the reservoir lane, passing the whole length of Llyn Egnant. Go ahead on a still distinct track, passing a waymarker, to a gate. Go through, and follow the fence rightward. The fence turns sharp right – go with it and follow it as it curves left. At a second, obvious, right turn leave the fence, which goes on to meet Llyn y Gorlan, to head for an obvious pass between small hillocks. Beyond is another similar pass. Go through this, then up and right over a ridge to reach Llyn Teifi (see ① Teifi Pools). Go around Llyn Teifi's southern

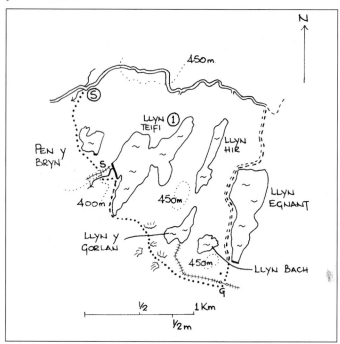

Walk 6: The Teifi Pools

end, following a concrete wall, which can be walked, towards the dam turret. Just before it, go left to follow and cross a stream to reach a stile over a fence.

Go over the stile, turning half-left beyond to reach the final dam wall, a construction more remarkable for its brutal pragmatism than its charm. Go round the last pool on its western side, avoiding its northern end which is very boggy. Instead make for a long, shallow grassy ridge to the left that leads back to the pull-in.

① *Teifi Pools*

The area of land around the pools is

reckoned to be the finest stretch of high, wild grassland left in the high mid-Wales plateau that has not dis-

Teifi pools

appeared under forestry. The land would originally have been forested with oak and birch, but this was cleared by the monks of nearby Strata Florida Abbey to make way for sheep. The Abbey – close to Pontrhydfendigaid, just a short distance south of Ffair Rhos, the village where the walker left the main road to reach the walk's start – is well worth visiting after completing the walk. It was begun in the 12th century, but became ruinous after the Dissolution. The Cistercians always chose pastoral sites for their houses, and Strata Florida is no exception, the ruins being wonderfully peaceful. It is thought that several Welsh princes lie in the abbey's cemetery. The 14th century poet, thought by many to be the greatest of all Welsh poets, Dafydd ap Gwilym, was also buried in the cemetery. The loss of the original oak and birch is sad, but the present wildness is to be preferred to regimented rows of conifer. Away from the pools navigation can be a problem, with the hills all looking a *little the same, the rock outcrops likewise, and the myriad small valleys and passes hindering rather than helping the walker. This geography does however produce ideal country for Wheatears and Buzzards, Ravens and Red Kites. In addition the bogs that surround and separate the pools prevent over-grazing and allow some really fine plants to maintain a hold. The walker will delight in finding his own favourite, but do look for the Bog Rosemary with its tiny, pink bell-like flowers.*

Southern Elenydd

South of the Teifi Pools the highland of Elenydd is very heavily wooded, especially at its centre where the Tywi Forest and its northern continuation stretch virtually continuously from a point about 4km (2½ miles) south of the pools all the way to the Llyn Brianne reservoir, and after a very short break on south to Llanwrtyd Wells. To the east of this huge forest area there is a fine moorland area around Drygarn Fawr, at 645m (2,116ft), the highest peak of Elenydd. Access to this area is not difficult, as the roads to the north – the Claerwen reservoir road – and south – the mountain road from Beulah Tregaron – are largely unfenced. The walking is rough, however, and there are a limited number of objectives and landmarks: it is land to walk across rather than around.

To the west of the area there is another huge forestry plantation, the Cwm Berwyn forest, north-west of which is Cors goch, Tregaron Bog. This peat bog, formed where a post-glacial lake once lay, is a naturalist's dream for its bog plant-life, butterflies, dragonflies, damselflies and migrating birds – over 160 species have been recorded. A path crosses an edge of the bog, but this gives the only access and barely constitutes a Best Walk.

Between the forests of Cwm Berwyn and Tywi there is a fine, if narrow, piece of moorland. Here is Soar y Mynydd, formerly one of Wale's most remote chapels. Excellent long walks link this site and others, crossing the moors and visiting the upper valley of the Doethie and Pysgotwr rivers, but again the general lie of the land and positions of access roads make short, circular walks difficult. South again are the valleys of the Gwenffrwd, Cothi and Tywi rivers forming an almost continuous circle around the high land of Mynydd Mallaen. These valleys offer some of the most beautiful wooded scenery in Wales – the drive from Pumsaint to Llandovery via Rhandirmwyn is one of the very best in Wales. The Cothi valley is reckoned by many to be the finest in Wales, though competition for that title is fierce and the Wye valley has sufficient admirers to ensure a victory in most polls. Nonetheless it is a fine valley, spoilt for the walker by access difficulties, few metres of its banks having footpaths. Sadly the same is true for most of the Gwenffrwd and Tywi valleys too, and we restrict ourselves here to two short walks that explore different aspects of the scenery of southern Elenydd.

WALK 7 | The Cothi Valley

The Cothi valley is a delight, a beautiful wooded valley running down from below the crags of Craig Branddu. Access to the river banks is severely restricted, but at a point near the village of Pumsaint the walker can get quite close, if only for a short distance. To produce a circular walk it is necessary to use roads to return to the start point, but these are quiet country lanes with views of the valley as good as any to be had, and offer the distinct advantage of a visit to the Roman gold mines of Dolaucothi.

Walk Category: Easy (1¾ hours) | Length: 6km (3¼ miles) | Ascent: 60m (200ft) | Maps: Landranger Sheet 146; Explorer Sheet 186 | Starting and finishing point: The village of Pumsaint on the A482 from Llandwrda to Lampeter. There is also a National Trust car park at the Dolaucothi Gold Mine, at 663 403, just off the main road, a little south of Pumsaint. This car-park is for visitors to the mine and so must be used with discretion. If it is largely empty, and you are intending to visit the mine after the walk, there would seem to be little harm

From the village go south towards the bridge over the Cothi, but before reaching it go left on a lane for Dolaucothi Farm. Follow the lane until another signed lane for the farm leads off right. The actual right of way does not follow this lane, but leaves the main lane about 150m further on. This 'real' path is not easy to locate, however, and custom and practice take the walker down the farm access lane. Where the lane splits take the left fork. At its end, go right, through the farmyard. Go down to a stile over a fence, noting the direction of a yellow arrow. Several stiles have these arrows and as the path is occasionally indistinct they are a useful guide.

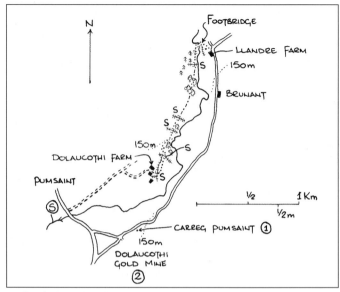

Walk 7: The Cothi Valley

Bear left after the first stile, following the left-hand hedge to another stile. Over this go left and up a steepish bank to where a marker post points to another stile. Beyond yet another stile there are two distinct, if not well-worn, paths ahead. The upper one goes along an avenue of trees, while the lower one goes down towards the river before rising again. Both paths meet at a stile beyond which the path, after descending towards the river, rises to go above a crumbling embankment. Care is needed here, particularly if the weather has been wet. Beyond this section, a piece of rough ground must be crossed to a footbridge over the Cothi. Here, at last, the full beauty of the valley is revealed. Over the bridge bear right with the fence, leaving it to go left of an old shed to reach a gate into Llandre Farm. Go across the yard and through another gate. Go right and follow the road to Carreg Pumsaint, to the left (see ① Carreg Pumsaint) and the entrance to the mine (see ② Dolaucothi Gold Mine). Continue to a road junction. Bear right and follow the road to the main A482. Go right for the least few metres into Pumsaint, pausing for one last look from the Cothi bridge.

① Carreg Pumsaint

Pumsaint is almost Welsh for five saints. Almost because although pum is the correct adjectival rendering of pump, for five, the Welsh for saint is sant, without the 'T'. It is clear however that the name is derived from an ancient legend that five Celtic saints set up a hermitage here in the Cothi valley. Of that original site nothing now remains and, strangely, there is no church within the village. This stone, Carreg Pumsaint, is said to have been a shelter for the saints, the hollows having been formed by their heads and shoulders. Sadly for this fine story there are only fours sets of impressions. Originally the marks were believed to be cup marks, a not-infrequent carving on menhirs, and the stone was assumed to be ancient. Today it is more widely believed that the stone has stood on the site for less than 200 years and that the impressions are from its use as an anvil in an ore-crushing machine, perhaps as lately as the 16th century.

The wooded mound beside the site is thought by some to be a Norman motte, but others contend that it is more likely to be a pile of mining waste! Slag heap not castle, anvil not miracle stone. So much for romance.

② Dolaucothi Gold Mine

Because of their experience with gold mining on mainland Europe – particularly in northern Spain where their techniques were described in detail by Pliny the Elder, techniques which match those employed at Dolaucothi – the Romans would have quickly realised the potential of the site here. The Roman extraction technique involved hushing (see Note ① of Walk 5(b)) to remove the topsoil and surface rock, a technique which required huge quantities of water. The water was taken from the Cothi several miles upstream and brought here by a brilliantly engineered aqueduct whose line can still be traced, in places, on the east side of the valley. Just south of Llandre Farm, passed on the walk, and again on the east

side of the valley, there was a tank that could hold one million litres (200,000 gallons) on water. Release of all or some of this scoured away the rock, the scoured flow being directed into channels that were partially dammed with gorse. The heavy gold fragments were filtered out by the gorse which was then burnt to release the metal. And in case all of this sounds very fanciful, the same technique was being employed to extract gold from near-surface veins only two centuries ago.

When the gold veins went underground the Romans would have followed them by trenching. To break up the rock more quickly than manual techniques could manage they lit fires to heat the rock, then cooled it rapidly with water to crack it. Close to the surface this technique is reasonable, but when carried out below ground it is a very hazardous procedure and, probably, slave labour would have been used. Water seepage would have been a problem once the mining was below the surface, and the Romans built waterwheels to pump the water out. It was the discovery of the remains of one of these wheels in the 1930s that confirmed Roman involvement at the site, though there had been local discoveries of superb gold jewellery.

From Roman times onwards there were sporadic attempts to find a lode at Dolaucothi, the technique employed being, as noted above, so similar that it is difficult to say with certainty which mining efforts are Roman and which are from times through to the 17th century. More recently there were half-a-dozen attempts to mine from the mid-19th century onwards. The last, and one of the most determined, was in the 1930s. Ironically this attempt failed, in 1938, shortly after the production of the first 100-ounce gold bar.

Today the Dolaucothi site is in the care of the National Trust. Visitors are kitted out with clothing, helmets and lamps and taken on a tour of the underground mine workings, a most interesting experience. For those not happy with enclosed spaces there is also a surface route, visiting the most important parts of the site. Refreshments are available.

The old winding tower, Dolaucothi

WALK 8 | Dinas

North of Pumsaint the visitor can follow the Cothi valley past Cwrt-y-cadno and under the crags of Craig Branddu to where the road leaves it as the river makes a right-angled turn. A footpath from near the telephone box here follows the river for a short way, passing Pwll Uffern-Cothi, Hell's Pool on the Cothi, thought by many researchers to be the source of water for the Roman aqueduct that fed Dolaucothi (see Walk 7). Beyond the point where the Cothi heads off there is a short rise and on the fall beyond, over Bwlch-y-rhiw, we have crossed the watershed: from here streams drain east to the Tywi not west to the Cothi. The first stream here is the Nant Melyn, which soon joins the Gwenffrwd. This river flows through land that was the scene of the joyously successful programme of the Royal Society for the Protection of Birds (RSPB) to save the Red Kite. A second RSPB site, and the start of Walk 8, is reached by crossing the Rhandirmwyn bridge just after the Gwenffrwd has joined the Afon Doethie.

Walk Category: Easy (1 hour) | Length: 3½ km (2 miles) | Ascent: 60m (200ft). | Maps: Landranger Sheets 146 or 147; Explorer Sheet 187 | Starting and finishing point: the RSPB car-park at 786 472 reached either by the route from Pumsaint as described above or from Llandovery. From Llandovery take the minor road northward for Rhandirmwyn continuing through that small village towards Llyn Brianne. The car-park is to the left, signed for the RSPB, after the church of St Paulinus has been passed. The car park is free to RSPB members but non-members are requested to put £1 in the honesty box. There is a picnic site on the right-side (as you enter) of the car park

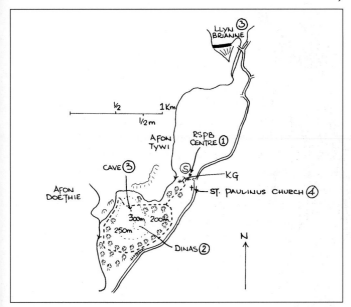

Walk 8: Dinas

At the bottom left-hand corner of the car-park a kissing gate leads to a raised wooden walkway that wends its way for around 400m to a wooded hillside (see ① RSPB Reserve). The walkway gives access to a boggy area that would otherwise be completely inaccessible. The visitor therefore has a very close view of some excellent bog plants. In exchange, the walkway can be a bit slippery if it is wet, especially on the uphill sections, despite the added metal mesh designed to provide a better grip. It also has occasional passing places because of its single-line traffic nature. As the walkway ends paths go left and right. One is the outward route, one the return. It is best, I feel, to go right first, to walk with the river, but as the river section of the journey is undoubtedly the best and many may prefer to go left, so as to leave it until last.

The boardwalk that takes the walker to the Afon Tywi

Rightward the river, the Afon Tywi, is soon reached, the route following a path which becomes rougher as it traverses the steep hillside of Dinas (see ② Dinas) above it. The river here is beautiful beyond superlatives, the craggy outcrops of Pen Rhiwbie adding a splendid backdrop to the view. Where the river makes a right-

angled turn to the left, a rugged path leads off to the left of the main path. Follow this to reach a cave (see ③ Twm Siôn Catti).

After a detour to the cave, continue along the main path, descending steps to reach more dramatic scenery where the rivers Tywi and Doethie meet. The path beyond is easier, and passes through delightful country, with the wooded hill to the left and, eventually, a fence on the right with a road beyond. When the walkway is reached again, retrace the outward route to regain the start.

Now to complete a good half-day the visitor can now visit a couple of local sites (see ④ Other places of interest).

① *RSPB reserve*

In London in the Middle Ages the rubbish-strewn streets were scavenged by a fork-tailed bird of prey, the Red Kite. Persecution and, later, hygiene forced the kite back to its country home, where it was further persecuted by gamekeepers and farmers. The bird is a nervous nester and disturbances at nest sites also took their toll. By the early years of the 20th century it was though that the kite was extinct in Britain, but a few pairs, perhaps as few as five or six, clung tenaciously to what remained of their range, the moorlands around the wooded nesting valleys of the Gwenffrwd and the Doethie streams. The birds' 'discovery' not so many years ago, when attitudes to wildlife among the general public were changing, caused a stir and the struggle to protect them and to increase their number became a cause célèbre.

The RSPB's part in the recovery, which involved the buying of Dinas in 1968, has been significant. Ironically the bird no longer nests in the two original valleys, but its range and numbers have increased. It is now seen over much of central Wales and has also been reintroduced to the Chilterns, which are also an ideal habitat: the Chiltern birds were actually Spanish in origin rather than Welsh. Visitors to Dinas always have a chance of seeing the bird. From a distance it is distinguished from the more common Buzzard by its deeply forked tail; when viewed from closer, by its colour – a gorgeous chestnut. Usually the bird is seen working the thermals above scarp slopes looking for its prey of small animals and birds. It also takes snakes, a habit that led one 19th century egg collector to warn of half-dead adders near its nest.

Over forty species of bird breed regularly in the sessile oakwoods and surrounding countryside of the RSPB's Dinas reserve. Chief among these are the Pied Flycatcher and Redstart, with Dippers and Yellow Wagtails near the Tywi. More information, and details on how to join the RSPB and so help it to continue its valuable work of protecting Britain's birds can be found on the car park information board.

② Dinas

Dinas means castle, although in Welsh it is frequently applied to natural rather than man-made fortresses. Here too the conical hill is a natural fortress, but with no direct evidence of its ever having been used as a defensive mound.

③ Twm Siôn Catti

Twm was born in the early years of 16th century to Catherine Jones of Tregaron. Catherine named him Thomas John, Twm Siôn in Welsh, and as he was illegitimate, Catti was added to his name: he was Cathy's Tom John. In reality Twm was probably a Protestant, a rebel against the Catholic laws of Queen Mary, and it is known that he fled to Geneva around 1550. He returned to Wales and was granted a Royal Pardon in 1559, marrying the widow of the Sheriff of Carmarthen

(after, legend has it, falling in love with her while he was stealing her jewellery during a highway robbery) and living to a respectable old age. The Pardon does not mention which crimes he was being pardoned of, and later, in the 18th century, the romantic ideal of Twm the Outlaw, a lovable rogue, grew up. Twm was portrayed as a Robin Hood figure, though with considerably more humour and less tragedy than the English outlaw. The cave roof has partially collapsed and crawling is necessary to gain access, though entry is barely worthwhile as there is little to see apart from some 19th century graffiti. The cave may also never have been a base for Twm, but the Dinas site certainly has the correct romantic image.

④ Other places of interest

St Paulinus church, near the car-park entrance, was built originally in the early 12th century, but has been much restored, chiefly by the Cowder family. It is a simple, dignified building more pleasing for its exterior and its position than for its interior. House Martins (refugees from the RSPB Reserve next door?) have taken over the eaves of the church.

About 2km (1 mile) north of the reserve is Llyn Brianne, a reservoir completed in 1972 and holding about 50,000 million litres 913,000 million gallons) of water. From the viewing point and picnic area just below the top of the dam the 'flip-bucket' water discharge looks very attractive. In addition to water flowing down the dam's spillway, some water is taken by pipe to the dam's base and turned up in the air to form a huge cone, not unlike a fountain for ping-pong balls at a fairground. In the right conditions a huge rainbow sits across the fountain and the visitor is wetted by the escaping spray. One advantage of the arrangement is that it oxygenates the water of the Tywi which helps the water life considerably.

Rustic seat for contemplating the Afon Tywi

The Radnor Forest

To the east of the Elan valley the mid-Wales plateau is dissected into smaller blocks by river valleys that hold the main access roads from South to North Wales. Around Llanbadarn Fynydd the block is slightly lower and more fertile, the land more cultivated and access slightly more difficult. This block is crossed by Owain Glyndwr's Way which visits Abbey Cwmhir, a magnificent – and historically important – monastic site, spoiled by poor preservation and indifferent planning decisions.

Southward is a second, smaller block, the Radnor Forest. Old Radnor, well set on a rocky ridge, has an ancient history, though when the Normans came they set their castle at New Radnor, to the west. This new site was the start of *The Journey through Wales* of Gerald of Wales and Archbishop Baldwin and, typical of the man, Gerald recounts a local anecdote about the castellan, or captain, of the castle in the time of Henry I. The captain spent a night in a local church, together with his dogs, and for this irreverence his dogs were driven mad and he was struck blind. After several years of misery he journeyed to Jerusalem hoping not for a cure, but for a chance of spiritual redemption. He reached the city during an upsurge in fighting between Christians and Muslims. He requested that he be strapped on to his horse and taken to the battlefield. He rode at the infidel army and was, of course, promptly killed. Gerald records, with satisfaction, that the captain's life thus ended with honour.

A later king, Charles I, stayed locally on the night of 6 August 1645 and was poorly fed at an inn called The Bush. Even the miserly ration of cheese he was offered was taken from him before he had eaten properly. The king, not amused, noted that the place should really be called Beggar's Bush, and so it still is, the name having transferred to a small hamlet a few miles north-east of New Radnor.

The Radnor Forest was originally a forest in the ancient sense of the name, a hunting ground, though lately the extensive forestry plantations on the north and south sides have given the old name a new meaning. It is a small, square area, no more than 6km (4 miles) on the side, with lovely little, partially-penetrating valleys. The highest points, Black Mixen and Great Rhos, are not on public rights of way – though Forestry Commission paths are gradually opening the area. Our walk uses one such path, visiting a delightful valley set in the heart of a forest area noted for its balance of tree species, to see a fine waterfall, Water-Break-Its-Neck.

WALK 9 | Water-Break-Its-Neck

Walk category: Easy (1 hour) | Length: 3km (2 miles) | Ascent: 40m (150ft) | Maps: Landranger Sheet 148; Explorer Sheet 200 | Starting and finishing point: At 186 598 at the end of a track from the A44 Llandrindod Wells to Kington road. The track turns off the main road about 3km (2 miles) south-west of New Radnor. There is a rough car park close to an information board soon after leaving the road. Further along the track there is another small, rough, car park. The latter shortens the walk, but fills quickly

From the first car park follow the track to the second. Now continue along the track, going downhill to reach an obvious track going off left in the dip by the stream. Follow this track, which eventually becomes a boardwalk, all the way to the waterfall. (see

Walk 9: Water-Break-Its-Neck

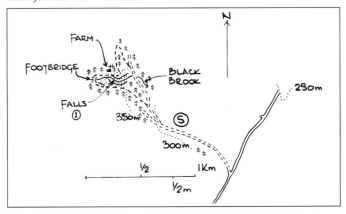

Water-break its-Neck. In dry weather the Falls is just a delightful trickle of water

Note ① Water-Break-Its-Neck). This fine, short walk returns along the same route, though it can be extended by following waymarked trails through the adjacent forest.

① *Water-Break-Its-Neck*

The elegantly named fall drops about 50m (80ft) over a sill of hard rock. In dry weather the stream, which has come only a short distance from its source, is a mere trickle and the waterfall is much less imposing than its name. After heavy rain however the volume is considerable and the falls are a fine sight. The valley below the falls is tight; the lack of sun and damp conditions have allowed a rich variety of mosses and plants to developed, some growing on exposed patches of rock.

The Pembrokeshire Coast National Park

To the west of Wales two arms of land enclose, pincer-like, a huge area of the Irish or Celtic Sea. The enclosed sea forms Cardigan Bay, the arms being the Lleyn Peninsula in the north and the wider, blunter snout of old Pembrokeshire to the south. The blunt snout is itself divided, the headlands near St David's and further south near Marloes enclosing St Bride's Bay, a miniature of the larger Cardigan Bay. South again the long inlet of Milford Haven, one of the world's finest natural harbours, separates the southern tip of the old county (an area from Pembroke to Tenby), from the main county bulk, creating what is virtually an island of land.

The rocks of Pembrokeshire are a geology lesson in themselves, there being representative masses of all the major geological eras from Pre-Cambrian to Recent, with a predominance of older rocks to the north and younger to the south. While the underlying geology affects the scenery it is at the coast that the layman gets his most obvious glimpse of the rocks. Southern Pembrokeshire has cliffs of Carboniferous limestone, an acid-dissolvable rock that has been etched by the sea into steep, jagged cliffs, constant weathering also producing a fine series of arches and towers. Further north the rocks are softer slates, easily weathered into smooth bays separated by cliffs of harder, unyielding rocks, some igneous in nature. The magnificent seascapes offered by these rock types, together with the pastoral beauty of inland Pembrokeshire and the existence of offshore islands that are important bird reserves led the National Parks Commission to designate the county's coast a National Park in 1952. The decision was far-sighted, the coastline here being rivalled only by that in Cornwall (in England and Wales). Apart from a small section around the busy ferry harbour of Fishguard, the whole of the coast is included in the Park. The decision to include all, rather than specific parts, means that the full range of varied coastal scenery is included, as too are the islands of Skomer, Skokholm and Ramsey, and the spiritual home of Wales, the cathedral village-city of St David's.

Equally far-sighted was the decision to deviate inland at one point in the north of the old county in order to include the Preseli Hills in the Park. These hills, though neither spectacularly beautiful, nor either high or extensive, are one of the most interesting prehistoric sites in Britain, the more so since the extraordinary discovery that some of the stones of Stonehenge were quarried from the range's eastern end.

Almost two decades after the designation of the National Park – the Coast Park was the fifth to be so designated and covers only 580 square km (225 square miles) - the Countryside Commission gave final approval to a long-distance footpath around the coast from Amroth on the old country border with Carmarthenshire to St Dogmael's on the old border with Cardiganshire. This is a superb walk, and while it does not visit all the interesting places in this remote and mysterious area, it does give an excellent view of a peninsula that the ancient Welsh knew as *gwlad hud a lledrith*, the land of magic and enchantment.

WALK 10 | St David's

The southernmost pincer that encloses Cardigan Bay comprises a broad headland, itself composed of a number of smaller headlands. St David's Head is the most northerly of these small promontories and southward from it is the magnificent sandy sweep of Whitesands Bay. Our route, a part of the official Pembrokeshire Coastal Path, takes the southern headland, which has few sandy bays – and access to those that there are is difficult – but offers superb rock scenery, a fine view of Ramsey Island, the advantage of walking around enough degrees of the compass to ensure that at least part of it is wind-free, and a chance to visit St David's itself, the spiritual heart of Christian Wales.

Walk Category: Intermediate (3½ hours) | Length: 15km (9 Miles) | Ascent: 90m (300ft) | Maps: Landranger Sheet 157; Outdoor Leisure Sheet 35 | Starting and finishing point: there are several. There is a car-park at 724 251 near St Justinian's, and another at 751 244 near St Non's. Better than either, and much bigger than either, is that used by visitors to St David's Cathedral

The walk can start by following the quiet country lane to St Justinian's, but this road walking can be avoided by taking the Celtic Coaster bus which operates hourly, in summer, from St David's. Whichever option you take, look out for the small hillock of Clegyr-Boia, to the left (south) about 1½ km from the centre of St David's. The hillock is topped by the remains of a hill fort (see ③ Porthlysgi). At the road end there is the first view of Ramsey Island (see ① St Justinian and Ramsey Island). Walk down to the Lifeboat Station and go left to gain the well-waymarked Coastal Path which is followed easily all the way around the headland. In

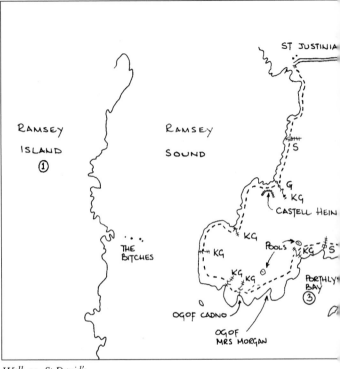

Walk 10: St David's

springtime this section of the coast is pure yellow with gorse which is packed tight against the path. There is so much that on still, warm days it can be smelt, a sweet, warm smell, vaguely reminding the walker of an exotic, cooked dessert in a five-star restaurant. Among the gorse there are Yellowhammers and Stonechats.

After about 800m (½ mile) Castell Heinif fort is passed, on the left, (see ② Castell Heinif), beyond which the walker is usually alone with the air and the view. After the headland of Penmaenmelyn, the most westerly point of mainland Wales, has been rounded there is a proliferation of paths near the bay of

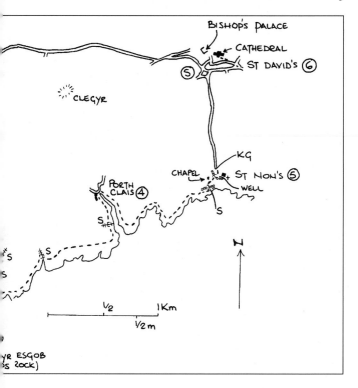

Ogof Cadno. At this point, and occasionally at other points along the way, all paths eventually rejoin, though to be absolutely safe take the one that is closest to the cliff edge. Beyond Ogof Cadno – *ogof* here being used in its sense of cavern, or steep-sided, rocky hollow, rather than cave, the usual meaning – is another rock-cut bay, the delightfully named Ogof Mrs Morgan. It is believed, but without true justification, that Mrs Morgan was associated in some way with the copper mines a little inland from here. Also inland is a small pond, the first of several, used for the irrigation of Pembrokeshire early potatoes.

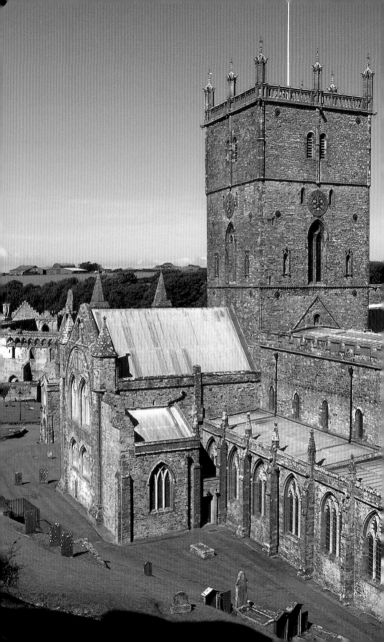

Ahead is a fine section of cliff, rounding Maen Llwydwyn to reach the sheltered bay of Porthlysgi (see ③ Porthlysgi). Here is a beach that is far enough from roads to be almost always empty. Offshore is Bishop's Rock, one of many so named. Beyond, the cliff is more vegetated to Porth Clais (see ④ Porth Clais), an infuriatingly long inlet. On this section the author was once startled by a young adder that crossed the path – perhaps you will be as lucky.

To compensate for its length, Porth Clais offers a superb sea-weedy smell. The walk can be shortened here as the Celtic Coaster also visits Porth Clais and can be used for a quick trip back to St David's. If you are continuing, there is excellent cliff scenery all the way to St Non's. As the retreat come into view, a stone stile to the left gives access to a grassy path that passes the chapel (see ⑤ St Non's) to reach the well. From the well a track leads to a car-park. Go left on the road to reach St David's, visiting the Cathedral and Bishop's Palace (see ⑥ St David's) before returning to the car park start.

① St Justinian and Ramsey Island

The harbour here is, in Welsh, Porthstinian, though locally it is frequently called St Justinian. The saint in question was a Breton hermit who, traditionally, arrived in Pembrokeshire towards the end of St David's life and acted as his confessor. He became Abbot of St David's Monastery, but was appalled at the lack of commitment of the monks there and left to become a hermit on Ramsey Island. Some of the monks followed him, but

became weary of his iron discipline and in a show of far from Christian compassion they cut off the saint's head. St Justinian's body picked up the head and walked with it across Ramsey Sound to this delightful harbour where the awe-struck locals buried both body and head, and raised a chapel. The chapel became a place of pilgrimage, but fell into disuse and disrepair. St Justinian's remains were then taken to St David's Cathedral. During the Civil War Cromwell's men stole the bells from the chapel, but their ship

St David's Cathedral with, beyond, the ruins of the Bishop's Palace

foundered in Ramsey Sound, during a storm. Today in stormy weather it is said that the bells can still be heard. The chapel is on private land.

Ramsey Island is probably named for a Viking settler, Hrafn. In Welsh the island was Ynys Dyfanog, Dyfanog being an early Celtic saint, but is now Ynys Dewi – St David's Isle – being by tradition the place where St David met St Patrick. The island has a long Christian tradition, going back several centuries before St Justinian, perhaps as far back as the second century. In the sound between the island and the mainland there is a vicious tidal race, with currents of up to 8 knots which makes it very dangerous, the dangers being added to by the series of sharp rocks that lie off the island's nearest point. These, The Bitches and The Whelps, are said to be the last remnants of a land bridge to the mainland. Legend has it that when St Justinian retreated to Ramsey he took an axe and broke up the land bridge behind him, but the axe became blunt and the last few strokes left slivers of rock behind. In fact Ramsey Sound is an ancient valley, ice-scoured in the last Ice Age and filled as the ice retreated. Today the island is a nature reserve and is

home to more than thirty nesting species. Climbing on the sheer cliffs is not permitted, but boat trips visit the island in summer, leaving from St Justinian where the beautifully sited lifeboat station was built in 1911 – for just £3000.

② Castell Heinif

The remains here are of an Iron Age fort. Typically these forts were built on hills and protected by an array of ramparts and ditches, but a promontory such as this had the natural advantage of being protected by sheer cliffs and the sea on two sides. A ditch and rampart section across the landward side thus gave total security for minimum labour. Near the fort is a superb natural rock arch.

③ Porthlysgi

This bay or harbour is named for Lysgi, an Irish pirate who is said to have landed here and killed the local Celtic chief, Boia. Boia gave his name to Clegyr-Boia passed en route *to St Justinian. Boia was head of a family who practised the ancient religion, perhaps druidism, and was in constant dispute with St David when he was establishing his first* monastery. A story tells of Boia's wife, stepmother to his daughter, taking the daughter, Dunawd, off to gather nuts, and cutting her throat as she rested. Where the blood touched the earth a spring, Ffynnon Dunawd, rose. This helped convert Boia to Christianity – though in truth the story has gross pagan overtones. Sadly, Boia's conversion did not save him from Lysgi.

④ Porth Clais

Porth Clais was the ancient harbour for St David's and must have seen a great deal of missionary and pilgrimage traffic even in pre-Norman times. The Normans built a harbour here, landing the stone for the cathedral and the lead for the roof, the present breakwater being constructed on their foundations. Later the harbour was used for the import of coal for use in the local gasworks. The works has now been demolished, the remains at the quayside being of earlier kilns used to supply local farmers with lime. The river that flows into the harbour is the Alun: near the bridge over it is the little that remains of Ffynnon Dewi – David's Well. Here the saint was baptised, a spring starting miraculously for the event.

At the baptism a blind man held David, and his sight was restored during the baby's immersion. Those familiar with the Mabinogion that wonderful collection of Celtic myth and legend through which drifts a tantalisingly elusive whiff of ancient folklore and which includes many tales of Arthur, will remember that Twrch Trywyth, the Irish boar which fought Arthur and his Knights, landed at Porth Clais after swimming from Ireland.

⑤ St Non's

St Non was the mother of St David, and tradition has it that the chapel ruins in the field are the site of the patron saint's birth. Non was the wife of Sant, a grandson of Cunedda, a local prince. Their home was here, close to the headland of Trwyn Cynddeiriog, Fury Point, and here, sometime between 462 and 502, St David was born. Tradition has it that the birth was during a thunderstorm though the birthplace 'shone with so serene a light that it glistened as though the sun was visible and God had brought it in front of the clouds'. During the birth a well sprang up nearby, St Non's Well. The Well was one of the most

On the Pembrokeshire Coastal Path

sacred in Wales and visited by most
pilgrims to St David's. It is said to
have miraculous healing powers,
being especially good for eye disor-
ders and for helping pregnant
women. The traditional offering to
the well was a pebble or pin – many
were found during a rebuilding and
re-dedication in 1951 – but today's
visitors favour a monetary gift.

After the birth of St David, St Non
went to Brittany and is buried at
Dinan in a chapel dedicated to her.
The chapel whose remains we see here
is of unknown date, but probably 13th
century. A fine brass from it, dated to
the late 14th century, was one of the
oldest and finest in Wales, but though
illustrations of it exist, the brass itself
was lost in the 19th century.

Nearby St Non's House was built in 1929 and taken over in 1939 by the Passionist Fathers who offer religious retreat and also training and renewal courses for people from all walks of life. The new chapel – to Our Lady and St Non -was built in the thirties, though it used many stones from other sacred sites, including St Non's Chapel. The window behind the altar is a fine pre-Raphaelite rendering of St Non.

⑥ St David's

Were it not for the cathedral the city of St David's – in Welsh Tyddewi, David's House – would be a village. Indeed, so small is the city, and so well hidden the cathedral, that it would be possible for an unfamiliar visitor to drive through without ever realising that the patron saint of Wales' cathedral was a few steps away.

From the 'village green', The Pebbles – so named because formerly it was pebbled – leads to Porth-y-Twr, the Tower Gate, a 13th century gateway to Cathedral Close. The close, containing the Cathedral and the Bishop's Palace, was completely walled, and much of the wall remains intact. Beyond the gateway the Cathedral comes into view, a magnificently compact, central-towered building, superbly set in the deep Alun valley and backed by the impressive ruins of the Bishop's Palace. The cathedral is reached down a flight of stone steps known as the Thirty-Nine Articles.

Very little is known about St David: the date of his birth is not known to better than forty years and even the date of his death, traditionally 1 March, is not really known with any certainty. As the son of a prince he would have received a good education and training as a priest. It is said that he was consecrated as a bishop in Jerusalem and the portable altar stone in the cathedral's south transept is said to have

been a gift from the Patriarch. St David spoke at the Synod of Brefi when tradition has it that a white dove flew down on to his shoulder. This explains the frequent representation of the saint with a dove on his right shoulder.

The first Cathedral on the site was destroyed, probably by Viking raiders, in 646 and successive raids destroyed further buildings through to the 11th century. Following the Norman Conquest the area became more stable, and rebuilding work commenced in earnest, though it was not completed until the early 16th century. Progress was not helped by the collapse of the tower in 1220, a collapse that destroyed much of the completed work.

Tours of the cathedral are offered in summer, and the interested visitor would do well to join one. Briefly, the building has a 12th century core, but much of the external work – in a curious purple sandstone – is 14th century. Inside, the cathedral is more elaborate, though very spacious and warm. The visitor will find the tomb of Edmund Tudor, father of Henry VII, whose remains were moved here from Carmarthen by his grandson, Henry VIII. Behind the high altar, an excavated recess was found to contain a number of bones, assumed to be those of St David and St Justinian. Formerly these were in a reliquary that pilgrims could touch, but may have been hidden at the Reformation. They are now held in an oak casket.

The Bishop's Palace beside the Cathedral is a magnificent building, both in position and construction. The palace is 13th and 14th century, but fell into disrepair after the Reformation, a decay hastened by the stripping of lead from the roof, the usual fate of monastic houses at the time. A tour of the palace, now in the hands of Cadw, the Welsh Heritage organisation, is very worthwhile, especially to see the wheel window in the eastern wall of the Great Hall, a superb feature.

WALK 11 | The Preseli Hills

The Pembrokeshire Coast National Park moves significantly inland only once, to enclose the Preseli Hills, old Pembrokeshire's only real upland mass. The hills are low by Welsh standards, barely making it to 500m (1650 ft), though there is a large area of land above 300m (1000ft), and measure only about 16km by 8km (10 x 5 miles), Nevertheless the area is of the greatest interest to the pre-historian, not least because of its associations with Stonehenge, and offers a superb series of vantage points.

When man was first making his mark on the landscape of Britain, with his stone axe factories and cromlech burial chambers, some of the country's valleys would have been inhospitable places, a land of wild boar and wolves. If a high ridge was bare of trees then that would be the place to walk, and it is believed that the east-west ridge of Preseli was crossed by an ancient track. The local axe factories – there are known to have been two from an analysis of the micro-structure of the rock, and though their exact locations have not been discovered it is probable that one lay near Carn Menyn – exported their work to Country Antrim and to 'Wessex', approximately due west and due east. The ridge trackway has long been known and has been given a variety of names by people anxious to explain away its origin. It was the Roman Road, though that it almost certainly was not; it was the Robbers' Road, a name given, perhaps, when times had changed and the valleys were more hospitable than the high land; and it was the Flemings' Way, improbable and more likely to be explained by the thoughts of the locals on those alien settlers (see Note 1 to Walk 2).

In fact the proliferation of ancient burial sites almost certainly gives the age. There are Neolithic cromlechs, most famously at Pentre Ifan on the northern flank of the hills, standing stones and alignments, and there are Bronze Age burial sites by the score. As with all later peoples, these early Pembrokeshire dwellers raised their churches and buried their dead beside the road.

The walk along the Preseli ridge is a fine one, especially in spring when the gorse and heather combine to form a carpet of yellow and purple, but the knowledge that you are following a trail that is, perhaps, 5000 years old adds to the attraction.

Walk Category: Difficult (4 hours) | Length: 16km (10 miles) for a single traverse of the length of the ridge | Ascent: 350m (1150ft) | Maps: Landranger Sheet 145; Outdoor Leisure Sheet 35 | Starting and finishing point: Unfortunately the Preseli Hills form a single east-west ridge a traverse of which leaves the walker a long way from his start point. The easiest way to overcome this is by the use of two cars parked one at each end of the ridge. There are car parks at 075 322 near Bwlch Gwynt, and also at 165 331 at the ridge's eastern end. Recently Preseli Green Dragon have opened bus services aimed at Preseli walkers. Though operating only on Tuesdays and Saturdays, and with only two services each day, these buses are excellent, linking Crymych and Newport and stopping at the Bwlch Gwynt car park. Walkers can therefore park at either end, using the bus to travel to the far end of the walk. For further information on this service telephone 0800 7831584 | Walkers not wanting to use the bus can shorten the walk. If the ascents of Foel Eryr and Foel Drygarn are omitted, the walker going only from Bwlch Gwynt to Carn Menyn and back will cover about 16km (10 miles)

From Bwlch Gwynt follow the obvious, and broad, track to the summit of Foel Eryr, the low peak to the west of the road (see ① Foel Eryr). Retrace the path to the Bwlch and now go east heading towards, then following, the northern edge of the Pantmaenog Forest. Beyond the forest some walkers may wish to head south to climb Foel Cwmcerwyn, at 536m (1760ft) the highest point on the Preseli Hills. It is topped by four Bronze Age burial cairns – the excavation of one of which revealed the remains of a cremation and a fine urn – but it is a disappointing viewpoint, the forest interfering with much of the view over 180 degrees of the panorama. Better is to continue eastward where good and indifferent tracks can be followed or ignored to reach Foel Feddau. This low summit, 467m (1530ft) high, is also topped by a Bronze Age burial cairn.

Eastward again the track is followed past Cerrigmarchogion (see ② Bedd Arthur) and on to Mynydd Bach. East again there is a shallow pass before the track rises to pass between Carn Bica and Carn Siân to reach Bedd Arthur (see ② Bedd Arthur). Ahead now the stony mass of Carn Menyn beckons, though the ridge walk takes a curving line northward rather than dropping into the valley of the Afon Tewgyll. Soon the flank of Carn Menyn is reached, and though the track itself does not visit the top there will be few walkers who will escape the lure of this most extraordinary of places (see ③ Carn Menyn).

Relocate the track and continue eastward: the edge of a forestry plantation is soon reached. There is a small rise, and from the top of it the walker can leave the track north-eastward, heading directly for Foel Drygarn. The valley is boggy however, and many will prefer to continue along the track to reach more solid ground for the visit to the last top on the route. This cross-valley variant goes past Carn Ferched, the Daughter's Grave, an obscurely named Bronze Age barrow. From Foel Drygarn's summit (see ④ Foel Drygarn) a clear path heads downhill, crossing a stream to reach the main track. Go over a stile and immediately turn left. Now where a track reaches the one you are on at a T-junction, turn right along it, following it to a road. The suggested car park is opposite, while for Crymych go left here, then right at the Y-junction to reach the A478. Go left for Crymych (see ⑤ Crymych).

---

① *Foel Eryr*

The 'mountain of the eagle' is

468m (1535ft) high, low enough to be insignificant in the list of Welsh peaks, but its position means that the view from it is remarkable. Perhaps the name derives from this eagle's eye view, the panorama extending north to Snowdonia, east to Mynydd Ddu, the first sandstone block of the Brecon Beacons National Park, south to Exmoor's Dunkery Beacon and westward across the Celtic Sea to the Wicklow Mountains. All on a clear day of course. More locally the view takes in virtually the whole of the new country – but old kingdom – of Dyfed. Indeed, so good is the panorama that it has been suggested that in prehistory the reason for Preseli's sacred nature was a belief that it represented the 'navel of the world', the centre of the local people's known universe.

Westward from Foel Eryr, the ancient walkers had to follow the beautiful Gwaun valley to reach Fishguard, one postulated harbour for Irish traders. Curving south (left) the track could have used Mynydd Cilciffeth – itself topped by Bronze Age cairns – arriving in the valley near Llanychaer – about 5km (3 miles) from Fishguard. Alternatively – and more probably – going north, the track reached Carn Ingli, topped by a large, but later, hill fort as well as numerous cairns,

Mynydd Dinas (more cairns), Carn Slani and Carn Fran.

② Bedd Arthur

This oval of twelve stones, at 131 324, is claimed to mark the grave of King Arthur. The dedication is hardly unique and indeed there is another site, Carn Arthur – where one boulder is perched on another – at 135 323 a few hundred metres to the south-east, though off the ridgeway, which is also claimed as the grave site. It is not unusual to find prehistoric sites associated with ancient gods and heroes, especially if the sites include megaliths. Clearly these huge standing stones could only have been raised by superhuman efforts. Arthur was the obvious superhuman, especially for a Celtic people who had been harried for centuries, first by Saxons and then by Normans, and were in need of supernatural help. In addition to the two named sites, Cerrigmarchogion – at 111 323, passed earlier on the ridgeway – is the Stone of the Knights, and Cerrig Meibion Arthur – at 118 310, to the south of the ridgeway – are two upright stones, the Sons of Arthur.

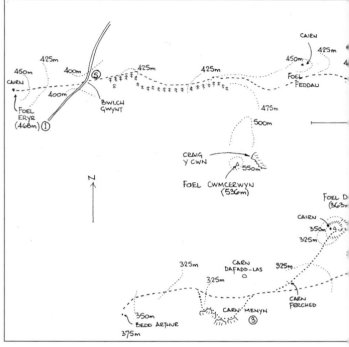

Walk 11: The Preseli Hills

The Preseli Hills also form the backdrop for some of the tales in the Mabinogion. One story has Arthur carrying out numerous 'impossible' deeds in order to secure a bride for Culhwch who is in love with Olwen, the daughter of a giant. One task is to take a comb and shears from the head of Twrch Trywyth, the giant magic boar whose landing place we saw on Walk 10 (see Note ④ of Walk 10).

Arthur and his men hunted the boar from the coast to Preseli where, after a chase over the ridge, it turned and fought near Foel Cwmcerwyn, mentioned early in the walk. The boar killed four knights, but was hunted on to the Severn where the comb was captured. The hunting of the boar also crossed Mynydd Ddu, where a river is named for the magic beast (see Note ① of Walk 15).

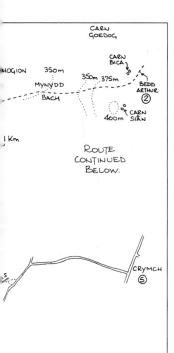

CARN
GOEDOG

CARN
BICA

HOGION   350m

350m 375m

MYNYDD
BACH

BEDD
ARTHUR
②

CARN
SIÂN

400m

1 Km

ROUTE
CONTINUED
BELOW.

CRYMCH
⑤

named for the three sons of Owen who decided to fight for their father's land, even before he had died(!), rather than divide it between them as the *Welsh gavelkind* required them to do. They made wooden clubs and fought all day on the hill, but as night fell no one had won. Eventually the father chose one son, sending the others to the kings of England and Scotland.

③ Carn Menyn

In its most complete form Stonehenge consisted of a circle of large sarsen stones coupled by lintels, an inner ring of smaller, unlinteled stones, an outer horseshoe of five huge, paired, linteled sarsens and an inner horse-shoe of nineteen smaller, unlinteled stones around a central 'altar' stone. In 1923 Dr. Herbert Thomas of the Geological Survey made the astonishing discovery that the inner circle and inner horseshoe stones were mostly of a spotted dolerite, known as bluestone, that forms the outcrops of Carn Menyn and Carn Ddafadlas here on the Preseli Hills' eastern end. Small numbers of stones were also found to be from nearby Foel Drygarn, and from Carn Alw, to the north of Carn Menyn.

In addition to Arthurian stories, many of the sites on Preseli have associated folk-tales. Carn Goedog, at 129 332, is the burial site of the black pig in the Welsh ballad of that name – Y Mochyn Du. Carn Sian – at 129 321, near Bedd Arthur – is said to have been the site of a chapel to St Silyn. But best of all is Carnedd Meibion Owen at 090 362, north of Bwlch Gwynt. This is

Bluestones, Carn Menyn

Various theories have been put forward to explain this discovery, which appears to belie the 'primitive' nature of Bronze Age folk and so beggared belief in the twenties, but the best of these, that a large number of stones had been 'accidentally' transported by ice during the last Ice Age, has now given way to the theory that the stones were transported by the Bronze Age Beaker Folk from Preseli to Milford Haven and floated to the mouth of the Bristol Avon. The stones were then floated upstream, hauled to the River Wylie, floated again, then finally hauled to the Stonehenge site.

Why? Salisbury Plain is still littered with sarsen stones of all sizes; there was no need to haul stones to it and certainly not from west Wales. Geoffrey of Monmouth, writing The History of the Kings of Britain *in the early 12th century, notes that Aurelius Ambrosius wished to raise a memorial over Celtic dead who had been killed by Hengist the Saxon. Merlin suggests that a suitable memorial would be the transfer of the Giant's Ring, a stone circle, from Ireland to the burial site on Salisbury Plain. When Aurelius points out that Britain is not lacking in stones, Merlin coun-*

ters by telling the king that the Giant's Ring stones have mystical powers. The king agrees and Merlin brings the stones, by sea and land. Hengist was a 5th century Saxon and Ireland is not Preseli, but Geoffrey could well have been picking up a folk memory that the bluestones were an ancient holy circle and were moved because of it. Preseli, indeed Wales, is short of stone circles. There is one, well set, but of small stones, that we shall see on Walk 17. Preseli has just one site, near Gors Fawr, at 134 294 to the south of Carn Menyn. That site has sixteen stones, each about 1m (3ft) tall, set in a not quite circular arrangement 20m (66ft) in diameter. However that Welsh shortage does not mean that there was not an important and large site on Preseli some 4,000 years ago. England does not have a large number of stone circles either, but it does have Avebury and Stonehenge. It therefore seems possible that there was once an important site on or near the Preseli Hills, and that it was moved to the then more important site on Salisbury Plain.

Cern Menyn would not have been a quarry in the modern sense. Rather it would have been a birthplace, large blocks of stone being naturally weathered by frost-cracking, from the outcrop. It is truly memorable to stand among the jumble of stones on the south side of Carn Menyn and to think that 4,000 years ago men laboured to move similar stones so many miles.

A bluestone, lifted into position by an RAF helicopter in 1989, has been erected close to the minor road which follows the southern edge of the eastern Preseli Hills, at 136 304.

④ Foel Drygarn

Foel Drygarn, the hill of three cairns, is indeed crowned by three Bronze Age burial cairns, quite the largest of their kind in west Wales. Later, during the Iron Age, the hill was fortified, three ramparts being visible. All over the summit plateau, within and between the ramparts, hut circles have been found. Because of its position, Foel Drygarn offers a superb view of the ancient ridgeway, and is well worth leaving the track to climb.

⑤ Crymych

Crymych itself is a straggling village with little to detain the walker. But to the east is a fine hill, Freni

Fawr, a last outcrop of the Preseli Hills.

Another tale from the Mabinogion is set here. In it the Roman Emperor Magnus Maximus hunts on its flank and camps on its summit. In Welsh the Emperor's name is Macsen Wledig, which explains the occasional name give to the hill, Cadair Facsen. The hill is also topped by Bronze Age cairns and reputedly home to a pot of gold. Usually such pots are buried beneath a cairn, but here it is just somewhere on the hillside. As is also usual, the pot is guarded, here by a hurricane-inducing phantom.

WALK 12 | St Govan's Head: (a) Castlemartin and (b) Bosherston Lily Ponds

In the south of Pembrokeshire there are superb limestone cliffs all the way from Castlemartin to the outskirts of Tenby, and these are followed by the Pembrokeshire Coastal Path. Though low by 'huge sea cliff' standards – the cliffs rarely exceed 40m (130ft), the limestone is in near vertical sheets and occasionally sculpted into stacks, arches, caves and sharply indented bays. There is interest all along this section of the coast: Lydstep Haven is a fine beach; Manorbier Castle, birthplace of Gerald of Wales, is superb; Stackpole Head is a fine jutting point and beside it is the romantically named Mowingword. But we go to the west, to concentrate on the area between Castlemartin and Bosherston. The Castlemartin cliffs have the disadvantage of forming part of the army's artillery range, though this does mean that access is reduced, leaving the cliffs quiet in the central section. Since access to the Castlemartin's cliff path is occasionally restricted by firing, an alternative is offered that visits the interesting lily ponds near Bosherston.

Walk Category: (a) Easy 1¼ hours from St Govan's to Stack Rocks);
(b) Easy (2 hours) | Length: (a) 6km (3¾ miles) from St Govan's
to Stack rocks; (b) 8km (5 miles) | Ascent: (a) Flat; (b) 60m
(200ft) | Maps: Landranger Sheet 158; Explorer Sheet 36 | Starting
and finishing point: The starting point for each walk is the car-park near
St Govan's Chapel, at 967 930. This is reached by continuing along the
lane from the B4319 near St Petrox that goes through Bosherston. For
Walk 12(a) use of this car-park doubles the stated mileage unless another
vehicle is available at the Stack Rocks car-park, at 925 945, reached by

another signed road off the B4329 near the Merrion army camp.
There is no public transport between the two car-parks.

(A) CASTLEMARTIN

If the artillery range is open there is a fine walk along the cliffs to Elegug Stacks and the Green Bridge of Wales. Sadly the permitted track does not allow continuous access to the cliff edge and is occasionally littered with unsightly debris. But with a little ingenuity and a decision to look the other way here and there, this a fine walk. *Within the range please do not touch any metal or odd-looking objects. Please also be careful if you have children, not only because of range debris, but because the cliff edges are sudden and unprotected, and very, very steep.*

From the car park go across to visit St Govan's Chapel (see ① St Govan's Chapel) before taking the westward track over the Castlemartin range (see ② Castlemartin). Soon there is a deep-cut inlet, Stennis Ford, beyond which the even narrower, darker, and more impressive, Huntsman's Leap is reached (see ③ Huntsman's Leap). Beyond, the track wanders inland occasionally, though numerous unofficial but beaten paths lead to the cliffs. The walker has rock climbers to thank for some of these access paths, the same climbers being responsible for the iron bars deeply embedded in the cliff-edge turf. These bars, which can trip the unwary – and this is no place to trip – are for belaying and abseiling. A metalled road is reached, but this is soon left in favour of the track which cuts off the headland of The Castle (see ④ Flimston). Westward the track reaches the oddly named Bullslaughter Bay, and at the bay's eastern end the view really opens out. The Elegug Stacks and Green Bridge come into view, in the distance, while close to hand the folded rocks and caves of the bay's cliffs are superb. Beyond the bay the track moves away from the cliff until Flimston is reached (see also ④ Flimston). This astonishing headland can be viewed at very

St. Govan's Head

close quarters, but do take great care, the cliffs are sheer and unprotected, and on the seaward side of The Cauldron the land bridge between sea and sea-filled hole is narrow. Beyond Flimston are the Elegug Stacks (see ⑤ Elegug Stacks) and the Green Bridge (see ⑥ Green Bridge of Wales) which is equipped with a viewing platform on its western side.

If no car awaits the walker at the Stack Rocks car-park, then the whole experience can be enjoyed again immediately, from the opposite direction.

① St Govan's Chapel

St Govan's Chapel is reached by a stone stairway. If you count the steps as you descend and then again of the way up, tradition says that you will not arrive at the same number. The chapel is named for Gobhan or Govan, 6th century Abbot of Dairinis in Wexford, Ireland, who

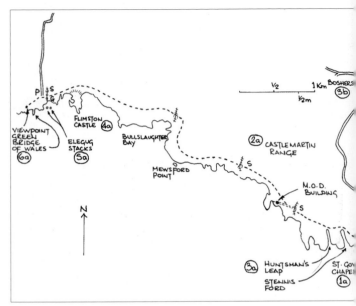

Walk 12: St Govan's Head

landed here having sailed across the Celtic Sea in his coracle. His hermitage cell was formed by cutting into the rock, and this cell can still be reached from the chapel built, of local stone, by his followers. The cleft in the cell's rock wall is said to have hidden Govan when raiders landed nearby. If the visitor enters the cleft a wish will be granted. The chapel's now empty bell-cote once held a silver bell which was stolen by raiders whose ship was wrecked on their escape. Sea nymphs rescued

the bell and returned it to the site, but to protect it against further raids they placed it in the middle of a rock near the well that used to supply the saint with water. If you find the right rock the bell will ring when you strike it. The well is seaward of the chapel and is probably original. Now blocked by stones, it was once revered for its healing powers.

An interesting tradition links the chapel to Arthurian legend. The lake at Bosherston is one of many that claim to be that into which Bedivere

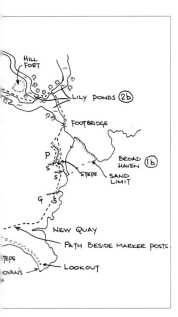

threw Excalibur, while Govan is said to derive from Gawaine, having been the final home of that knight after Arthur's last battle.

② Castlemartin

The Castlemartin range is one of the largest in Wales and is used for the firing of live ammunition. The merits or otherwise of such ranges need not be discussed here, but the choice of Castlemartin does have a link with history, the Castlemartin Yeomanry being the only regiment to have been awarded a battle honour for a battle on British soil. In 1797 1,400 Frenchmen – half of them reluctant conscripts, and led by a British-hating American – landed at Carregwastad Point near Fishguard. They captured a farm, got drunk on stolen liquor, were frightened to death by the sight of the Fishguard women-folk who, because of their red cloaks and tall hats, they thought were Guardsmen, and surrendered to the Yeomanry with little resistance on the following day.

③ Huntsman's Leap

This narrow cleft has also been called Adam's Leap, but the more common name derives from a local tale that a rider being pursued along the cliff by robbers or creditors jumped the chasm to escape them. He stopped and dismounted to see what he had crossed and died of fright.

④ Flimston

On this section of the coast there are two promontory forts. The Castle is the earlier, dating from around the 2nd century AD. Below it, at low tide, the boilers of the Ionian, a wrecked World War I troopship, can be seen.

Flimston Castle is later, dating from the 4th century AD, though the name is later still, deriving from 'Flemish town' because tradition has the Flemish settlers arriving here in the early 12th century. The Cauldron, the most obvious feature, is a huge hole produced by limestone folding and erosion. The sea pounds into the hole through a natural arch that can be crossed, and offers a spectacular view of nature in the raw.

⑤ *Elegug Stacks*

The stacks are named for an ancient, seemingly non-Welsh, word for the Guillemot, an apt name in view of the number of the auks that nest on them. The bigger stack is Elegug tower, the smaller, more elegant one is Elegug Spire. Each can be climbed – out of the auk-nesting season – by routes at about VS (Very Severe)

grade. The descent, from indifferent abseil anchors, is awesome. In addition to Guillemots there is a large breeding population of Razorbills and Fulmars.

⑥ *The Green Bridge of Wales*

In the evolution of the coast by marine erosion, caves in the cliff are the earliest sign. If the rock formations are appropriate, two back-to-back caves erode to form a natural arch which eventually collapses to leave sea stacks. Locally there are fine examples of the process. Flimston has one robust, early arch, while the Elegug Stacks are the remains of one or more arches. The Green Bridge is a superb, slender midway point. Soon, on a geological timescale, the arch will collapse to leave a single stack. The Green Bridge can be crossed, but crossers should be cautious. It is narrow and precarious and in high winds downright dangerous.

(B) BOSHERSTON LILY PONDS

If the Castlemartin range is closed this walk offers a fine alternative. In its early stages it crosses another part of the range, but one that

Cliffs near Castlemartin. Misty days can enhance the magical nature of this area of Pembrokeshire

Bosherston lily pond

is more frequently open. Even if it is closed Bosherston village can be reached and used as a car-park so that the lily ponds and Broad Haven can be visited.

From the car-park visit St Govan's Chapel (see Note ① of Walk 12(a)). From the top of the chapel steps take the metalled track that follows the cliff edge closely to the coastguard look-out at the southern tip of St Govan's Head. This cliff area is favoured by climbers so please be careful to avoid the iron bars banged into the cliff-edge to act as belay and abseil points. The path must now be retraced, for two reasons: firstly as the official coastal path is the only right of way, and secondly to avoid the deep incut from the old harbour of New Quay.

The official path is marked by white posts to another car-park at 975 939 where steps by the National Trust building lead down right to the beach of Broad Haven (see ① Broad Haven). Cross the back of the beach, heading almost due north, to where the stream runs on to it. Follow the stream, then cross it by footbridge and turn left, keeping a lake on your left hand. The lake (see ② Bosherston Lily Ponds) is crossed by a grassy bridge. At its end go left to reach a stone causeway that crosses the lake again. From the causeway a path leads to another causeway that crosses the lake for a third time. Between the causeways there is an inaccessible Iron Age fort on the hill to the right on a spur of land between the lake arms.

From the end of the last causeway an easy path leads to Bosherston church. Go along the lane to the village road (see ③ Bosherston). There turn left and follow the road back to the start.

① Broad Haven

The St Govan's Broad Haven is occasionally referred to as Broad Haven South to avoid confusion with the other beach of the same name near St. Bride's. The name Stackpole, applied to the nearby headland, the extensive dune system to the east of the ponds and the estate on which the ponds lie, is believed to be Norse in origin, probably from stac, a rock pillar – those in the bay, no doubt – and poler, an inlet. The dunes at the back of the haven have grown since the damming of the ponds at the end of the 18th century and their ecology is fragile. Please be careful not to destroy either the plant life or the dunes themselves. The dunes are held together by marram grass, but there are lovely little patches of colour in summer, the blue Viper's Bugloss and the pink Restharrow. Overshadowing some of the flowers is Sea Buckthorn, a tallish, fast-growing shrub with a mixed reputation. Its berries help feed migrating birds, its sharp thorns deter people and so protect the dunes, but it does suffocate lower, less hardy species.

② Bosherston Lily Ponds

The Stackpole Estate was owned by the Scottish Earls of Cawdor until it was transferred to the National Trust, and it was members of this family who dammed the valleys of three streams bound for Broad Haven to form the lily ponds. The ponds cover 32 hectares (80 acres) and are nationally important because of the *underlying calcareous marls. The lakes hold Perch, Roach, Tench and Pike – as well as Excalibur, see Note ① of Walk 12(a) – while the surface is often criss-crossed by dragonflies. The ponds are famous for their lilies, which are at their best in June. The ponds are popular with birds, especially Heron, Coot, Moorhen, Mallard and Mute Swans. The lucky visitor will also see the electric blue flash of a Kingfisher, while in winter there is a good collection of winter migrants. Over twenty species of duck have been recorded, including Goosander, Smew and Goldeneye.*

③ *Bosherston*

Bosherston is a tiny village: a few houses, a pub, a tea-shop and the church of St. Michael and All Angels. The church is 13th century Norman, and has a fine stained glass window of St Govan. It also has a good hagioscope, or squint, a passage in the chancel wall that allowed those in the side chapel to see the altar. Outside is an old cross, perhaps as old as the church itself.

The Gower Peninsula

To the west of Swansea is an oblong block of land measuring about 25km by 14km (15 by 8 miles) that appears to have been tacked on almost as an afterthought. The Gower Peninsula is a land of scenic contrasts. To the south there are superb limestone sea cliffs, as well sculpted as any to be found in the southern part of the Pembrokeshire Coast National Park, while to the north there are broad sand and mud flats at the edge of the Burry estuary. Linking the two in the west is Rhossili Bay, with one of the finest stretches of flat sand in Wales, enclosed by the interesting horns of Worm's Head and Burry Holms. Inland the Gower is flat, pastoral land with few raised sections. Indeed the best 'upland' area is Rhossili Down which backs the sand of Rhossili Bay. The Peninsula was designated as an Area of Outstanding Natural Beauty in 1957, the first such designation in Britain.

Gower – the locals will quickly tell you that you can say the Gower Peninsula or Gower, but that you must never, ever say the Gower – was a strange land. Heavily 'Normanised' in the early years after the Conquest, the peninsula was always less Welsh than the surrounding land, the locals an island race proud of their independence, which they guarded jealously. The sea coast, particularly the jagged rocks of the south and Rhossili Bay, were notoriously dangerous in the days of sail: in places the ghosts of wrecked and drowned mariners must stand shoulder to shoulder on the cliff tops. Some of the wrecks – and the number is staggering, whole books have been written on Gower shipwrecks – were 'assisted' by false lights, though it must also be said that many of the locals were as brave in their assistance of sailors in distress as others were keen on helping cause the distress.

Of late, Gower has seen a revival of its fortunes as a holidaying centre, but its roads are too narrow, its bays too small and too difficult to reach for it ever to suffer from overburdening hordes. It is to be hoped that its cliffs will long remain the haunt of the Fulmar, that most marvellous of all fliers, and the interested walker.

WALK 13 | Rhossili

At the extreme south-western tip of the Gower Peninsula there is an excellent diversity of scenery in a small area: open downland, a huge sandy beach, limestone caves, and an extraordinary geological feature. Our walk visits all of these. Rhossili, because of its position, is windswept, but our walk traverses from south-facing to west-facing cliffs and so guarantees some shelter if there is a steady blow. Rhossili has always been popular with the tourist. Dylan Thomas, a man of nearby Swansea, wrote a famous short story. 'Who do you wish was with us?' about a visit here, a story still as true now as when he wrote it.

The walker on this route can visit Worm's Head, but should bear in mind that the 'causeway' to the Head is only open for 2½ hours each side of low tide. Please check the times for crossing before setting out.

Walk Category: Intermediate (3½ hours) if Worm's Head is visited | Length: 9km (5½ miles) | Ascent: 200m (650 feet) | Maps: Landranger Sheet 159; Explorer Sheet 164 | Starting and finishing point: The car-park at the south-western (far) end of Rhossili village, reached by taking the B4247 that leaves the A4118 Swansea to Port Eynon road at the village of Scurlage

Go back along the village road, passing the church to your left (see ① Rhossili Church). Now take a lane to the left, following it to a gate. Go through this. There is track ahead which contours around the lower flank of Rhossili Down to reach a road from where a track heads back, uphill to Sweyne's Howes. This is not too satisfactory a route: better is to bear right, following the wall and then continuing straight up on to reach The Beacon.

Continue along the ridge to reach Sweyne's Howes (see ②
Rhossili Down).

Retrace the route to The Beacon, but then bear left to follow a
track to a covered reservoir (on the right) from where a track
heads south-east to reach a lane. Turn right along the lane to
reach the main road (the B4247). Cross and turn left, passing
'Mewslade View' to reach a lane on the right. Follow this to a
gate. Go through and walk ahead to reach a path fork (see ③
Rhossili field system). The left branch soon reaches the cliff above
Mewslade Bay. The cliff top path is clear now, going around Fall
Bay to Tears Point where a wall can be followed as it heads
towards the headland close to Worms Head. The old coastguard
lookout at the headland is now the property of the National Trust.
The Trust formerly leased it to the Countryside Council who had
an Information Centre there. The lease expired and the Trust have
now taken it back: at the time of writing it is empty, but the Trust
intend to open it soon, also as an Information Centre.

From the headland a descent can be made to the shore. This is
worthwhile even if the land bridge to Worm's Head is flooded as
the rock pools abound with life. Hermit crabs are especially
numerous here. If tides permit the crossing can be made to
Worm's Head (see ④ Worm's Head). Do be cautious: there is no
path, the way is laborious and over slippery and jagged rocks on
which it is easy to slip. The author once witnessed a helicopter
rescue from the causeway's centre, the winchman just beating the
tide to a visitor who had broken an ankle sliding off a patch of
seaweed. The Worm is in three parts, a path taking the left-hand
side of Inner Head to reach the Middle and Outer Heads.

Regain the headland and return to the village along the broad
cliff-top path. The view of the cliffs, from which limestone was
quarried and also burnt in local kilns, and of the broad sweep of
Rhossili Beach (see ⑤ Rhossili Beach) is superb. The return passes
a National Trust shop where information on tides, a necessity for
crossing to Worms Head, is available.

① Rhossili Church

The church of St Mary the Virgin, though built in the 14th century, is Rhossili's second church, the first lying beneath the sands of The Warren, below the village. That first church, revealed in great detail by severe floods in 1979/80, was built in the mid-12th century. The present church is a stout Norman construction, notable for a memorial to P.O. Edgar Evans, a local man, who died with Scott on the retreat from the South Pole in early 1912. Evans was a man of immense strength and was chosen for that reason, but he became exhausted from sledge-hauling and on 17 February became the first of the five-man team to die.

② Rhossili Down

On a good day, one with a reasonable inshore wind, the top of the Down and the sky all around is filled with hang-gliders, Rhossili being one of the country's foremost areas for the sport. At 193m (632ft) the Down offers sufficient height, and its sea face deflects the wind to give excellent up-draughts. The Down's summit, known as The Beacon, offers a superb panorama stretching from St Govan's Head in Pembrokeshire to Devon's Hartland Point. The summit area contains no fewer than fourteen Bronze Age burial cairns erected, it is believed, by the Beaker Folk, the people who, it is also believed, moved Preseli bluestones to Stonehenge. The cairns are estimated to be 3,500 years old.

Sweyne's Howes, or Swine Houses (there are two houses about 100m apart), about 1km (~½ mile) north of The Beacon, are older. Though having a Norse name they are in fact Neolithic burial chambers – cromlechs – of a basic design and they are, perhaps, 1000 years older than the cairns on The Beacon.

③ Rhossili field system

A look at Explorer Sheet 164 reveals an astonishing network of field boundaries near Rhossili. This area, known as the Viel or Vile, is good limestone farmland, in contrast to the poor, acidic Old Red Sandstone of the Down, and was divided into strips by low grass banks. Village folk were allocated strips at random to ensure a mix of good and bad land, and as later fences and walls were placed along the grass banks – which can still be seen – the old

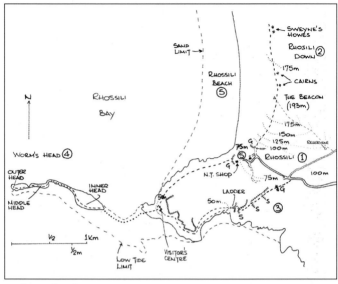

Walk 13: Rhossili

field pattern remains, one of the best survivals of a medieval field system in Britain.

④ Worm's Head

The name 'worm' is Old English, often taking the form 'orm', and means a dragon or, more likely in this case, a sea serpent. The Head is an outlier of harder rock, an eccentric form of the sea stacks we met on Walk 12(a). In form it is two rock masses, the long, tent-shaped Inner Head being joined by a long ridge of

rock and a rock arch – known as the Devil's Bridge – to a second mass. This second mass is half-divided by a thinned section into the Middle and Outer Heads. On Outer Head there is a blow hole, air being compressed in a lower sea cave and puffed piston-like out of a vertical fissure. Outer Head is a noted bird sanctuary, especially for Razorbills, Guillemots, Kittiwakes and Fulmar, and as a consequence access to it is prohibited from 1 March to 31 July each year.

Not surprisingly the Head has attracted local tales. One such is that the Celtic saint Cenydd – after whom Llangennydd, at the northern end of Rhossili Down, is named – set adrift, as a child, on the sea in a wicker cradle, was rescued on to the Worm by seabirds. Leland, the Elizabethan traveller, was convinced that the Worm was a magical doorway to another world, claiming that there was a 'Hole at the Poynt of Worme Heade, but few dare enter it, and Men fable there that a Dore within the spatius Hole hathe be seen with great nayles in it'. Leland also claimed that there was a secret passageway beneath the sea from the Head to a place in Carmarthenshire.

On a calm, sunny day the Worm is a friendly place, but with a stormy sea running it seems far from hospitable, yet there is evidence of a hill fort on Inner Head, and bones found in a cave on Outer Head suggest a Mesolithic presence.

⑤ Rhossili Beach

Between Worm's Head and Burry Holms there is an 8km (5 mile) arc of beautiful sand, one of the finest of Welsh beaches. But in the days of sailing ships Rhossili Bay could often be a far from happy place. Facing due west it could be an unavoidable target for a windblown ship, and many have come to grief. The most famous is actually the least well documented. In the latter part of the 17th century a gold-ladened Spanish galleon came ashore, though nothing definite about the ship, its crew or its position is known. A very low tide in 1807, and another in 1823, allowed a large number of silver dollars to be found far out, but on each occasion the incoming tide prevented an exact position of the hoard to be marked. Today the 'Dollar Ship' is another treasure trove awaiting its lucky finder. More obvious are the timbers of the Helvetia that can be seen at the southern end of the bay. The timbers are all that remain of a barque that grounded in November 1887. Luckily all the crew escaped unharmed, though five men were sadly lost when a salvage ship was retrieving the Helvetia's cargo of wood.

The Brecon Beacons National Park

The Brecon Beacons National Park, a huge Park covering a total of 1330 square km (519 square miles) was designated by the National Parks Commission in 1957. Most people, when considering the Park, remember only the Old Redstone masses. In one sense that is hardly surprising since the four distinct masses of Mynydd Ddu, Forest Fawr, the Beacons themselves, and the Black Mountains are the Park's most distinctive features and represent a sizeable proportion of its area.

But there is other, and varied scenery, within the Park's boundaries. To the south of Forest Fawr, the limestone sheet that once capped the whole of the Old Red Sandstone still exists. The low-lying area is cave country, the sculpted limestone also producing waterfalls. The whole is enclosed in a typically lush limestone vegetation, the trees being especially good. Eastwards there is another area where the original limestone capping sheet is still present. At Llangattock, however, the limestone forms a high and exposed plateau which, while still being very good for caves, offers little chance for vegetation. Only where there have been quarries is there such plant life, as the old, steep quarry walls offer some protection.

Between the limestone of Llangattock and the sandstone block of the Beacons and the final, easternmost sandstone block of the Black Mountains runs the river Usk in its wide, gentle valley. The National Park is a generous shape with none of the exclusion zones of, say, the Snowdonia Park, or even the Pembrokeshire Coastal Park, and encloses the Usk from its source right through to Abergavenny. The valley is a good one, providing the best

Sgwd Clun-gwyn

access to all areas of the Park and some secluded, if somewhat less easily accessed, river scenery.

In the walks that follow the main mountain masses are dealt with individually. Despite its wholeness in the geological sense, the Park's masses are unique and, because of the Park's dimensions, quite well separated.

Mynydd Ddu

The most westerly of the sandstone masses of the National Park is also the biggest and, in a sense, the most poorly defined. There is a scarp slope, indeed the scarp slope is one of the steepest and most continuous in the Park, but it is set in the middle of a raised plateau and has not been weathered into distinctive peaks. As a result, the horns, as the angles of the scarp slope are called, though high, are not prominent summits as are, for instance, Corn Du and Pen y Fan.

Old Red Sandstone is a soft rock, as the weathered, well-rounded peaks indicate, and was easily sculpted by ice. Here the ice sheets scoured hollows at the bases of two of the steepest sections of scarp slope. In each case the glacial moraine created a dam when the ice retreated, trapping water to form corrie lakes. Llyn y Fan Fach lies at the foot of the northern scarp slope, a mysterious sheet of water, a home to fairies, while Llyn y Fan Fawr, the larger lake, as the name implies, but only just so, lies at the foot of the long eastern-facing scarp slope and is a friendlier stretch of water.

North of the scarp slope there is a raised plateau of land that has been forested. Here the Usk rises (from the Usk reservoir), the plateau ending where it meets the river's valley, and that of the Afon Gwyddarig that flows west to Llandovery. The real surprise lies south and west of the scarp slope, where the dip slope is an undulating plateau that extends over a huge area. This area, a tangled mass of shallow peaks and valleys, rock outcrops and bogs, is a true wilderness, the only real wilderness in the Park for all its high land. This moorland plateau is trminated by the Tawe valley, the river rising near Llyn y Fan Fawr and flowing close to a remnant of the limestone capping sheet. The sheet here is riddled with caves, to such an extent that it represents one of the finest caving areas in Britain.

WALK 14 | Carreg Cennen

At its extreme eastern edge Mynydd Ddu falls away into the Cennen valley. On the other (north-western) side of the valley there is a rugged mass of limestone completely dominates the valley's upper reaches. This naturally defensive position was, not surprisingly, exploited by the castle builders and today the gaunt ruins of a 13th-century castle top the mass. Our route circles the mass, gaining the best of the views, not only of the castle, but toward the edge of Mynydd Ddu.

Walk Category: Easy/Intermediate (2½ hours) | Length: 8km (5 miles) | Ascent: 250m (800ft) | Maps: Landranger Sheet 159; Outdoor Leisure Sheet 12 | Starting and finishing point: the castle car-park at 668 194, reached by a minor, signed, road from the hamlet of Trapp, itself reached by minor roads from the main A483 Llandeilo to Ammanford road

From the end of the car-park furthest from the castle, go through a gate into Castle Farm. Turn right and go through another gate, next to a barn, then downhill across a field to reach a stile on to a lane. Turn left. Ignore a stile on the right, then, when a house – Pantyffynnont, to the right – comes into view look for a stile in the hedge to the right: it is waymarked with a castle symbol (as is the whole route, though occasionally not too well) and signed for Llwyn-bedw. Go over and steeply down the field on an obvious, but indistinct, path to a second stile. Beyond this the grass is even steeper and more slippery to another stile. Go over to reach a footbridge crossing the Afon Cennen. Go half left and up to a stile, beyond which go steeply uphill, parallel to the trees/fence on the left, towards the buildings of Llwyn-bedw. Aim for the

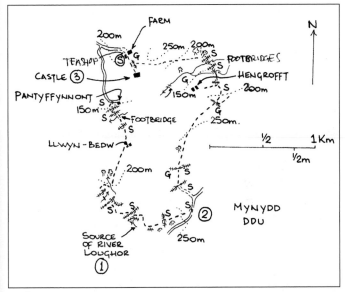

Walk 14: Carreg Cennen

right-hand side of the buildings and go right along the unfenced farm lane.

The lane passes superb oak trees, crosses a cattle grid and ford and then goes round a hairpin bend. Go over another cattle grid to reach a signed stile to the left. Go over and along the track, crossing a footbridge and another stile. Beyond, the route leaves the stony track on a less distinct path – the yellow marker on the last stile gives the direction – to another stile. Beyond this the source of the Loughor can be reached on the right (see ① source of the Loughor).

The way forward is the obvious stony track that becomes grassy and trends leftwards after a left-right swing. Beyond another stile the path becomes indistinct: keep to the left of the obvious hollows, heading across the field to where the field's right retaining wall becomes a fence. There a stile leads to a minor

Carreg Cennen Castle

road. Go left. To the right now is the final western edge of Mynydd Ddu. On its unfenced edge are a number of pillow mounds (see ② Beddau'r Derwyddion).

Where the lane goes right, go left on a stony track to reach a stile. Ahead there is a distinct grass track to another stile beyond which the path becomes indistinct. Maintain direction downhill to meet a fence from the left: continue to reach a gate on to a track at a hairpin bend to the right. Follow the track around another hairpin bend, this time to the left, then cross a signed stile on the right. Follow the enclosed lane to the Afon Cennen, crossing two bridges and stiles to join a path. Turn right on this, but almost immediately go left, uphill to reach a gate to the castle grounds. The castle is to the left (see ③ Carreg Cennen Castle), while the car park start is to the right.

① *Source of the Loughor*

The river's source is reached over a stile. The river rises from a cave, a tribute to the limestone country, and is a delight.

② *Beddau'r Derwyddion*

The long and grassy mounds on the edge of Mynydd Ddu are known in Welsh as Beddau'r Derwyddion, the Graves of the Druids, and do indeed look like burial mounds. In fact they are artificial rabbit warrens, built by locals to act as a source of fresh meat when times were hard.

③ *Carreg Cennen Castle*

Carreg Cennen is such an obviously defensive feature that it is difficult to imagine that there has been a time when it has not been fortified. The first known occupation, however, was Roman, coins having been found on site that date their time here to the 1st to 4th centuries AD. Any later fortification by the Celts would have been obliterated by later stone-built castles, first mention of which is in 1248. At that time the castle was owned by the local Lord of Dinefwr, Rhys ap Gruffydd. That is an inter-esting ownership, especially to the visitor more used to the huge castles of North Wales, for it implies that Carreg Cennen was built by the Welsh, rather than by the Normans. Another interesting feature is that despite its apparent impregnability the castle changed hands no fewer than ten times in the ten years from 1277 to 1287 during disputes between local lords. A closer reading of the evidence from the feuds suggests that they were, in part, between the Welsh and the Normans, and that Lord Rhys – Rhys's lordship was granted by Henry I – actually won the castle from a Norman owner and lost it to another. Certainly it was a Norman owner, Sir John Gifford, who remodelled the castle along the lines we see now. For a century the castle remained quiet, a quiet rudely shattered during the rebellion of Owain Glyndwr.

Glyndwr's rebellion was a vicious affair with each side breaking the unwritten rules of medieval warfare by looting monasteries and burning the land. Here at Carreg Cennen, Glyndwr was asked by Sir John Scudamore, the castle's keeper, to grant safe passage to the womenfolk. Glyndwr refused and besieged the castle for months.

Later, during the Wars of the Roses, the Lancastrians used the castle, but surrendered it to a Yorkshire force after the battle of Mortimer's Cross in 1461. The Yorkists employed local labour, at a cost of £28, to dismantle the bulk of the defences, making the castle useless as a fortress and forming the ruin we see today.

One interesting feature of the ruin is the existence of a natural cave in the limestone beneath it, reached by a man-made passage through the rock. The cave was a source of water for the occupants, though it was not their sole source, and was also, presumably, a good cold storage room. It has also been suggested that the cave might have been 'included' in the castle design to prevent its use by an attacker. As there appears to be no access to it from outside this seems most unlikely. The visitor can borrow a torch to inspect the passage and cave at the entrance shop.

WALK 15 | Deepest Mynydd Ddu

Behind the steep scarp slope of Mynydd Ddu the dip slope is a vast moor with swallet holes, bogs, streams and acres of good walking. The country is not easy to traverse, a place for the dedicated map and compass walker, or the walker with a GPS, but deserves inclusion because of all the walks in the book the walker is most likely to remain a solitary animal on this one.

The walk is difficult and should only be attempted by the fit and those well-versed in the use of map, compass and GPS. In very wet weather the conditions under foot can be atrocious and the route is not recommended at all if the visibility is poor.

Walk Category: Difficult (4 hours, for a one-way traverse) | Length: 14km (9 miles) for a one-way traverse | Ascent: 500m (1650ft) | Maps: Landranger Sheet 160; Outdoor Leisure Sheet 12 | Starting and finishing point: No reasonable round trip can be made from the walk, though it is possible to return around the scarp edge — more than doubling the stated distance. For a one-way traverse the walker will need support, being dropped off north of Llanddeusant and collected near the Dan-yr-Ogof caves. The start point is at 778 237 where there is a convenient dropping-off point. This point is reached along a narrow lane that goes south from close to the church in Llanddeusant. The finishing point is the car-park at the Dan-yr-Ogof caves reached from the main A4067 or the Gwyn Arms Public House at 846 166

From the start point follow the lane south-eastwards – the left fork of the Y-junction reached from Llanddeusant – and follow it through a gate and around a right-hand bend. A distinct green path leaves the lane leftward: this is the actual right-of-way, but it soon becomes lost among undergrowth and fences, and it is better

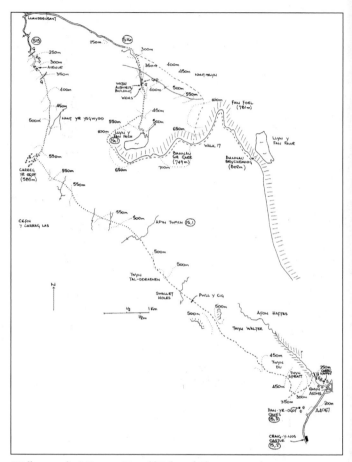

Walks 15 and 16: Deepest Mynydd Ddu and Llyn y Fan Fach

to follow custom and practice, and to take a much more distinct
track to the left 100m or so further on. This track leads to a gate
on to the open moor. There is no path ahead now, the route going
true south, then bearing slightly west to the top of the obvious
peak, Carreg yr Ogof, where a shattered limestone pavement that

has created a mass of splintered stones and the occasional 'wall' section. The limestone is delightful on this Old Red Sandstone mass. There seems to be no evidence of the cave of the name ever having existed.

From Carreg yr Ogof the walker is on his own, the footpath marked prominently on the maps being a good deal less prominent on the ground. It is however best to follow its approximate line to pick up the final track. Do not, therefore, go up Garreg Las to the south – although the ascent of this peak does allow the whole route to be scanned, that not being possible from Carreg yr Ogof, but descend south-eastwards on a bearing of 130°, continuing around the wide descending flank of Bannau Sir Gaer to reach the Afon Twrch at 802 198 (see ① Afon Twrch). Climb to Twyn Tal-Ddraenen, at 805 190, then continue south-east to cross the Afon Giedd – named for Bwlch y Giedd, the pass crossed by Walk 17 – crossing a stream to reach Pwll y Cig at 812 185. Beyond the Pwll a more distinct track is followed south-east.

The track skirts the edge of Waun Fignen-felen, a bog of mystical proportions that remains wet even in the driest of summers, but is not the mother of rivers. Indeed the Afon Haffes forms the eastern edge of the bog before running down Cwm Haffes. We go the same way, passing the poorly defined hills (*twyns*) of Walter, Du and Spratt. 'Du' is black, 'Walter' is interesting but 'spratt'? Beyond Twyn Spratt the path joins a distinct, raised green lane that goes across the hillside from right to left (south-west to north-east) at the boundary of the Dan-yr-Ogof site. The site fence must not be crossed, but from it there is a fine view of Craig-y-nos Castle (see ② Craig-y-nos). Go left instead, following the new track to the Afon Haffes which is crossed with a difficulty that depends entirely on the weather. In the valley below there are warning signs about the dangers of the river in flood. Go down the river's left bank to a gate in the wall, left, and follow the track beyond to and around the farm of Cerrig Haffes, to a stile on to the main road. To reach the Gwyn Arms, cross the main road and take the path opposite to reach a lay-by (the old road). The Gwyn Arms is to the left.

To reach the alternative end point, go right along the main road to reach the well-signed car-park at Dan-yr-Ogof (see ③ Dan-yr-Ogof).

---

① *Afon Twrch*

On Walk 10 we visited the landing spot in Wales of the magic boar Twrch Trywyth whose hunting is part of the story of Culhwch and Olwen in the Mabinogion, *the book of Celtic legends. Culhwch, the hero of the story, is set a large number of seemingly impossible tasks by Olwen's father, a giant, including the obtaining of a comb and scissors from Twrch Trywyth's head for the giant to attend to his hair. Culhwch seeks King Arthur's help and Arthur agrees, explaining that the boar is a king turned into a pig for his sins. The boar comes ashore and is hunted across Preseli and Mynydd Ddu, and on to the Severn where the comb is obtained. The hunt then continues to Cornwall were the shears are finally won. Eventually all of the tasks are completed and Culhwch wins Olwen. The river here is named after the magic boar, a reminder of the chase across the moorland.*

② *Craig-y-nos*

Craig-y-nos Castle was built in the grand style as recently as 1842 and was bought by the most famous opera singer of her day, Adeline Patti, in 1878. Madame Patti was born of Italian parents in Madrid in 1843 and when she came to Craig-y-nos she was at the height of a glittering career that took her all over the world. Craig-y-nos was her retreat, though countless distinguished guests visited it and she gave frequent performances of her greatest roles in the little theatre she had built within the castle. To these performances the local Welsh folk were often invited. In the grounds of the castle she created a pleasure ground, with an ornamental pond and an artificial lake complete with island. In 1898 her second husband died and the following year, at fifty-six, she married a twenty-nine-year-old baron, causing a local sensation. She died in 1919 and the castle was bought as a sanatorium. It later became a hospital for

The western edge of Mynydd Ddu from Carreg Cennen

the elderly. It is now a restaurant and function centre. The grounds now form the Craig-y-nos Country Park and are open daily all year.

③ Dan-yr-Ogof

The Tawe valley near Craig-y-nos is now famous as a caving centre, Ogof

Ffynnon Ddu being one of the longest and deepest caves in Britain, with more than 50km (30 miles) of explored passage that reaches a depth of over 300m (~1,000ft). This cave lies to the east of the river. In 1912 two local brothers, the Morgans, discovered another cave on the western side, Dan-yr-Ogof. To date more than 15km (10 miles) of this cave have been explored. The initial section has been opened to the public and is one of the finest, if not the finest, show cave in Britain. The extraordinary beautiful features have names, but they are a good deal less fanciful than most. There is an underground pool, originally crossed by the Morgans in a coracle, and a fine waterfall. Best of all is the Cathedral, the largest chamber of any show cave in Britain and quite breathtaking.

WALK 16 | (a) Llyn y Fan Fach and (b) The Llyn y Fan Fach Horseshoe

Our second Mynydd Ddu walk reaches the smaller of the two Van lakes that nestle below the inverted tick of the Mynydd Ddu escarpment. It is a straightforward walk, a gentle introduction to the area, reaching a brooding stretch of water associated with one of the next remarkable folk-tales in Wales, but can be extended in spectacular style.

Walk Category: (a) Easy (1¾ hours) (b) Difficult (4 hours) | Length: (a) 5km (3 miles) (b) 10km (6 miles) | Ascent: (a) 250m (800ft) (b) 700m (2,300ft) | Maps: Landranger Sheet 160; Outdoor Leisure Sheet 12 | Starting and finishing point: The village of Llanddeusant lies to the north-west of the escarpment and is reached by narrow, but delightful, country lanes from the north, the east and the west. For those approaching from the west, several lanes reach the village form the A4069 Brynamman to Llangadog road. From the north Llanddeusant can be reached by an excellent, but slow, series of lanes from Llandovery through Myddfai. The best approach is from the east, where a lane from Trecastle (Trecastell) on the A40 Brecon to Llandovery road, reaches Pont ar Hydfer and then, after a short forest section, crosses a high moorland plateau that lies at the base of the escarpment before reaching Llanddeusant. The view to the steep scarp slope is an appetiser for the walk. From Llanddeusant a lane signed for the lake heads off eastward, and this can be followed to a small 'car-park' that has been excavated just short of the Water Authority sign which warns that no unauthorised vehicles may pass the spot

---

(a) From the 'car-park' our route follows the Water Authority track southward and uphill. The lucky walker here will see Dippers in

Mynydd Ddu from the north

the stream, while only the very unlucky will not see Meadow Pipits. In spring they are entertaining, with their steep climbs and parachuting descents as they stake their territorial claims, and fine songs. Near an Authority building and a small complex of weirs the track is blocked by a locked gate, but a gap in the wall, left allows the gate to be bypassed without the need for climbing. Continue to the lake (see ① Llyn y Fan Fach). The easy walk reverses the route to regain the start.

(b) The horseshoe walk takes the skyline above the lake. From any convenient point north of the Water Authority building, strike out rightwards across the moor to gain the obvious ridge which is then followed to the top of the cliff at the western end of Bannau Sir Gaer. Continue along the cliff edge. A very steep descent can be made back to the lake close to the summit of Bannau Sir Gaer, but please be careful. The grass is treacherous when wet, and can be polished by the sun so that it is no less treacherous when the weather is dry. Great care must be taken, but the descent can be made. As the base of the slope is neared, bear left towards the lake as a concrete conduit runs around the base and can only be realistically crossed near a sluice at the lake end.

The better alternative is to continue over the summit, then down to the col of Bwlch Blaen-Twrch. Now climb up to the top of Fan Foel. Descend by heading east of north, but soon bear left-wards to follow the shallow valley of the Nant Melyn, staying on the left side of the stream to avoid having to cross it later. The Nant Melyn runs into the outflow stream from Llyn y Fan Fach. Rejoin the track from the car park at the confluence, turning right to reverse the outward route.

① *Llyn y Fan Fach*

Many years ago, a local young man called Rhiwallon regularly took his sheep to the shores of the lake for pasture. On one trip he was astonished to see a girl emerge from the water and sit on a rock at the lake's edge. Rhiwallon fell in love with her immediately and offered her his lunchtime bread. She refused to take it, and refused unbaked bread the next time that Rhiwallon found her at the lake edge. Finally Rhiwallon's mother baked him a different sort of bread which the girl accepted. She agreed to Rhiwallon's offer of mar-riage, but told the lad that he must first ask her father's permission and that she would leave him if he struck her three times. The next day Rhiwallon returned to the lake and was astonished to find the father there with six daughters, all identical. His love wiggled a toe so he could distinguish her when her father said Rhiwallon must be able to pick the right girl if he was to marry her, and the couple departed for their new life together.

Over the years three sons were born but Rhiwallon did strike her three times, each time just a tap to correct what he saw as incorrect behaviour – she laughed at a funeral and cried at a wedding – and on the third occasion she left him to return to the lake. She returned to visit her sons, to the oldest of whom, named Rhiwallon after his father, she taught

The outflowing stream from Llyn y Fan Fach. In the distance is Bannau Sir Gaer

her secret healing ways with herbs
and other natural things. Rhiwallon,
the son, became a famous local healer
and passed the tradition on, giving
rise to a line of local healers known

as the Physicians of Myddfai,
Myddfai being a small village a little
way north of Llanddeusant.

On the face of it this is just
another folk-tale, the legend of the

Lady of the Lake, similar to many other local tales and, indeed, a few stories in the Mabinogion. *However a delve into some of the odder features of some versions of the tale suggests a much more intriguing possibility. In some Rhiwallon and his family visit the lake girl's people – who are small and dark whereas his people are tall and blond – and their market, because there are many of them living in or sometimes on the lake. Rhiwallon cannot understand the girl's language and occasionally the unlucky strikes he must not make, may not be with iron rather than not being with the hand.*

When the tall, blond Celts came to Wales about 3,000 years ago they encountered a Bronze Age people who were smaller and darker. They would not have been able to understand these people, and may have had difficulty in distinguishing them, after all, is it not true that all foreigners look alike? The Bronze Age people of Britain occasionally built their villages on rafts, as with the famous lake villages of Somerset, and to such a culture an iron sword or implement would have been a formidable, a fearsome thing, so fearsome perhaps that touching it would have

been taboo. And the older culture might well have been skilled in herbal medicines to an extent that amazed the Celts. Bearing in mind all these ingredients – but bearing in mind also that what we are dealing with here is speculation not fact – then the tale could be a most remarkable folk memory of the meeting of two cultures. If that is so then the meeting would appear to have been a happy one, an intermixing rather than an annihilation, an opinion reinforced by a horde found in Glamorgan that contained both bronze and iron objects.

One thing that is certainly true is that there was a line of doctors from Myddfai. A quick investigation of the churchyard there reveals the names of several, and it is known that from a Myddfai-born Aberystwyth doctor of the mid-19th century an unbroken line stretches back at least 600 years. In addition there is a medieval book of remedies from the Physicians. It is full of homely (and good) advice on diet, even if some now seems dated – 'If thou desirest to die, eat cabbage in August'! Some of the remedies appear grimmer than the diseases they are meant to cure, for instance what could possible be worse than

taking a medicine made of chicken droppings, gunpowder and brimstone? To cure toothache a powder was made from ground-up newts and 'those nasty beetles which are found in ferns during summer' and applied to the tooth.

Taken together, the story of the Lady of the Lake and the Physicians of Myddfai offer one of the most intriguing legends to be found anywhere in Wales.

The folk tradition of the story has a peculiarly enduring nature. It is said that until very recent times local folk would visit the lake on the first Sunday of August to await the return of Rhiwallon's bride.

Bannau Sir Gaer above Llyn y Fan Fach

WALK 17 | The Horns of Mynydd Ddu

This walk visits the larger of the two Van lakes as well as reaching and following the scarp edge for an impressive view of Llyn y Fan Fach, the smaller lake visited on Walk 16. The walk also visits a small, but interesting megalithic site, one of a good number that exist on the eastern flank of Mynydd Ddu.

Walk Category: difficult (4½ hours) | Length: 14km (9 miles) | Ascent: 750m (2,500ft) | Maps: Landranger Sheet 160; Outdoor Leisure Sheet 12 | Starting and finishing point: At 853 215 on the minor road that links the A4067 Ystradgynlais to Sennybridge road with Trecastle. This road, going north from near the Dan-yr-Ogof caves, rises towards Bwlch Cerrig Duon. Before reaching the summit of the pass there is a prominent pull-off to the left of the road, overlooking the young river Tawe

From the start point follow the road southward, crossing the infant Tywi and climbing briefly to reach the megalithic site of Cerrig Duon (see ① Cerrig Duon) from which the road pass is named. From the site the walker must cross rough moorland heading north-westward towards Llyn y Fan Fawr. From the southern edge of the lake a stream, Nant y Llyn, flows down to reach the Tawe. This stream gives the line if it is reached, its left bank being followed all the way to the lake outflow (see ② Llyn y Fan Fawr).

Cross the outflow and take the obvious rising path that crosses the steep scarp slope to reach the skyline ridge at Bwlch y Giedd. The scarp ridge here is impressive. Southward, its long sweep, known as Fan Hir – the long crest – is a formidable barrier to the walker. As a digression it is also a very fine walk, being reached

The Afon Tywi, crossed early in the walk

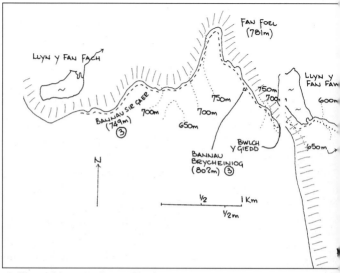

Walk 17: The Horns of Mynydd Ddu

from the Tawe valley, but further south than our starting point. Northward, above Llyn y Fan Fawr, the scarp slope is equally steep and formidable. It is no surprise that on this little-walked block of the Brecon Beacons, where the walker is often alone on the trackless moor, a well-trodden route appears, to take him to Bwlch Giedd.

The climb to the depression in the Fan Hir ridge offers magnificent views across the lake. At the Bwlch, go right (north) to climb to the shelter and trig point of Bannau Brycheiniog (see ③ The Horns of Mynydd Ddu). Continue along the scarp edge to reach Fan Foel, from where the edge nips back on itself, turning south and then west to take the walker to Bannau Sir Gaer (see, also, Note ③), reached after a sharp descent and ascent to and after Bwlch Blaen-Twrch.

From Bannau Sir Gaer's summit it is worth continuing along the scarp edge to a point above Llyn y Fan Fach (see (Note ① of

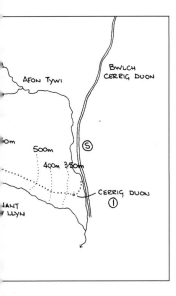

Walk 16) before reversing the route to Bannau Brycheiniog and Bwlch y Giedd, and descending the ascent route to Llyn y Fan Fawr. From the lake's northern tip the source of the River Tawe can be reached. The river arises not from the lake, but from the moor a couple of hundred metres east of its north shore. In very wet weather the dry land gap between the two is tenuous, but in dry weather it is real enough. Despite the fact that Llyn y Fan Fawr is such a large body of water and an obvious river source, only the small Nant y Llyn flows out of it. As the walker follows the young Tawe downstream – and so returns to the starting point – he or she will notice that the moor to the east of the lake is, in fact, mother to many streams, the Tawe being a sizeable river long before the Nant y Llyn reaches it.

① Cerrig Duon

There are few stone circles in Wales, and even fewer megalithic alignments, which makes Cerrig Duon – the Black Stones – an interesting site. The circle is about 17m (55ft) in diameter and consists of about twenty stones each 500-750cm (1½ – 2½ft) high. At the north-eastern edge of the circle stands the single 2m (6½ ft) Maen Mawr – The Big Stone. It is believed that the stones of Cerrig Duon (and of Saith Maen a short distance to the south) are Bronze Age. That makes the sites at least 4,000 years old, which represents an almost unbridgeable time gap, so that there seems little chance that we will ever understand the precise reason for their erection or what rituals were carried out at them. Knowing that merely adds to the appeal of these marvellously atmospheric, but enigmatic sites.

② Llyn y Fan Fawr

Llyn y Fan Fawr is a 'friendlier' stretch of water than its smaller neighbour, this being due in large part to its position on the sunny side of the hill. Assuming that the legend of Llyn y Fan Fach (see Note ① of Walk 16) is just that, a legend, it is easy to see why that lake was chosen in preference to this, the larger one. On the scarp walls above the lake, where the sandstone is rich in lime, there is a fine collection of unusual plants, including Mossy and Burnet Saxifrage, Great Burnet and Roseroot. There are also fine outcrops of Green Spleenwort.

③ The Horns of Mynydd Ddu

The names Bannau Brycheiniog and Bannau Sir Gaer mean, respectively, the Horns of Breconshire and the Horns of Carmarthenshire. Until the redrawing of county boundaries, the two peaks stood on either side of the border dividing the two old counties. Today the peaks still stand on either side of the boundary line that divides Dyfed and Powys. The name derives from the resemblance that the sharply turning scarp edge bears to a horn, a resemblance that is vague from a distance, but slightly better defined when the walker is on the edge itself.

Forest Fawr

Between the masses of Mynydd Ddu and the Brecon Beacons lies Forest Fawr, an upland plateau with several distinctive peaks, bounded by the A4067 to the west and the A470/A4059 to the east. There are some access problems to the peaks, for although the rounded hump of Fan Fawr can be ascended along clear paths, the way on to Fan Gyhirych, a far more impressive peak, is much less clear.

It is to the south that the area comes into its own. Here the limestone that once capped the entire area still remains. It is carboniferous limestone, the dissolvable, cave-producing rock, and produces the extraordinary spectacle, in the valleys of the Hepste and Mellte rivers, of whole rivers being swallowed. For many tens of metres at a stretch the rivers flow underground, the valley floor being dry with the occasional swallet hole allowing the visitor to hear and sometimes even glimpse the river. The limestone has occasionally been eaten away to reveal the underlying Millstone Grit. This harder rock, also occasionally exposed by geological faulting, produces waterfalls which serve to enhance the scenery still further. And as a last treat the country is low-lying so that the normal rich, lime-loving flora grows in abundance.

WALK 18 | Caves and Waterfalls

This magnificent walk, scenically one of the finest in the list, is straightforward, if a little arduous on occasions, and links together the best of the waterfalls on the Hepste and Mellte rivers, as well as visiting one of the most memorable cave entrances in Wales.

Walk Category: Intermediate (2 hours) | Length: 8km (5 Miles) | Ascent: 150m (500ft) | Maps: Landranger Sheet 160; Outdoor Leisure Sheet 12 | Starting and finishing point: The car-park at 928 124, reached by turning left off the road that runs south from Ystradfellte, about 1½ km (1 mile) south of the village. Ystradfellte itself is reached by a fine, but narrow, road that links Heol Senni to Pontneddfechan and the A465 Heads of the Valleys road. The Heol Senni to Pontneddfechan road passes between Fan Nedd and Fan Llia, two peaks of Forest Fawr, and follows the Afon Llia, a major tributary of the Afon Hepste. There is a fee for use of the car park

From the car-park a steep, occasionally unstable path of polished stones leads to a stile, on the left, over which is the River Mellte and the cave entrance of Porth yr Ogof (see ① Porth yr Ogof). The cave entrance is easily reached by way of a conveniently located rock shelf and is big enough to allow light to penetrate some way into the cave, so that the intrepid boulder-hopper or the well-shod can get far enough in to see the White Horse (see Note ①), and to enjoy the view back out through the entrance to the Mellte valley. But please take note of the warnings at the cave entrance, which are repeated in Note ①.

The Afon Mellte

From the cave the walker must return to the car-park and then go back to the road. Cross the road and take the left-hand of two paths, an obvious and well-worn trail. To the right a signed path (for cavers) leads past several swallet holes (see ② Swallet holes and clints and grykes) to a rocky platform above the superb resurgence cave of the Afon Mellte (see, also, Note ②). Beyond the resurgence is a beautiful section of limestone pavement (see, also, Note ②). The main path descends to a meadow, then mainly stays close to the river, going through two kissing gates to reach a footbridge. The path beyond the footbridge leads to a viewpoint of the first waterfall.

However, the walk does not cross the bridge (except as a detour), continuing along the path which climbs steeply. To this point the walk has been through fine open country with excellent flower-filled water meadows ringed by trees. Ahead now is a superb section of deciduous wood, a fine setting for the waterfalls. At the top of the climb, bear left to reach a path fork. Take the left fork, passing the occasional waymarker post to reach a cross-roads of paths. Turn right along the path signed for Sgwd yr Eira, following the waymarker posts through delightful woodland to reach another right turn, Go steeply downhill, bearing right to reach steps which lead down to the falls (see ③ Sgwd yr Eira).

Go back up the steps and turn left, following a waymarked path to reach a signed path, on the left, for Sgwd y Pannwr and Sgwd Isaf Clun-Gwyn. Follow this path to reach the first falls (see ④ Sgwd y Pannwr), continuing on to reach the second, which is seen at its best by carefully following a rough path (see ⑤ The Clun-gwyn Falls).

To continue, retrace your steps back to the main path (at the sign for the two waterfalls). Turn left and soon you will reach the point on the outward journey where you forked left. From here the last falls (see Note ⑤) is reached by a short detour to the left. To return to the start, retrace the outward journey.

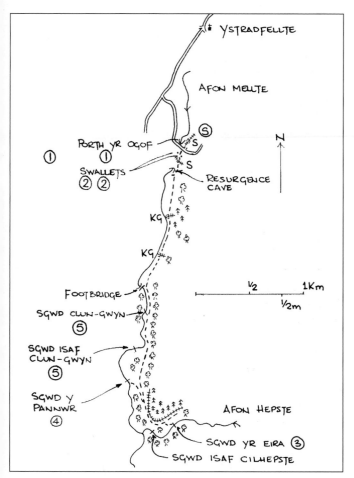

Walk 18: Caves and Waterfalls

① *Porth yr Ogof*

Porth yr Ogof – the Door of the Cave – is the largest cave entrance in

Wales, a slot of an entrance some 15m (50ft) wide and 5m (16ft) high. It is one of a large number of entrances to an extensive and still relatively unexplored cave system. The casual visitor can, with a little care, penetrate quite a long way inside the cave, certainly far enough to see the Pool of the White Horse. The pool is named because of the resemblance to a horse's head of a series of calcite streaks on its back wall. Legend has it that long ago a Welsh princess rode into the cave to escape a pursuer whose intentions towards her were a good deal less than honourable. Her horse stumbled and fell, and both horse and rider were drowned. The horse's head was struck on the wall as a sad reminder.

The legend has one link with reality: the ease with which it is possible to drown in the cave. Experienced cavers with full equipment, including wet suits, and a knowledge of cave-diving have died here because of the speed with which the system fills with water after heavy rain. The Mellte – the name, aptly, means lightning – is a curious river occasionally running underground along its length, and is prone to rapid rises in level if there is a storm on Forest Fawr. In times of flood the cave entrance can be almost filled with water and escape becomes impossible. Please be careful: a missed footing could be disastrous in the dark of the cave if the river is moving quickly and rising rapidly.

② Swallet holes and clints and grykes

The carboniferous limestone underlying the waterfall country is soluble in acid, and both the Mellte's water and rainwater are mildly acidic. Limestone is also a sedimentary rock, with a system of regular joints that offer a penetration path for water. Over the course of millions of years the water eats away the rock, faster in some places than others because of variations in penetration rate, to form a variety of natural features. The most obvious are caves, and Porth yr Ogof (see Note ① above) is the best example. Here an underground tunnel system has been carved out, the river disappearing from view for several hundred metres and returning to the surface in spectacular style at its cave resurgence.

Between the cave entrance and exit there are several swallet holes, where the dissolving process has been active vertically with a single joint being preferentially attacked to produce a funnel-shaped hole. Such holes can lead to river-dissolved cave systems, and some of Britain's best pot-holes are entered by way of swallets. The name is a Mendip (Somerset) one – and so preferred by the author – but is only one of many given to the feature, swallow hole, pot-hole, sink hole, shake hole. Even on the Mendips it is a local name, being confined to the northern section: to the south of that area the holes are known as slockers (pronounced slow-kerr). The underground river can occasionally be glimpsed, and most certainly heard, down one swallet, but do be cautious as the hole edges are unstable.

Where the attack on the limestone is less concentrated the weathering is more even, producing a limestone pavement where the joints have been more uniformly dissolved. Here steps of limestone, known as clints, are separated by deep slots, known as grykes. The best section of clints and grykes in Britain is that above Malham Cove in the Yorkshire Dales, but the section here is a good, if short, example.

③ Sgwd yr Eira

Sgwd yr Eira, the Fall of Snow, is a superstar waterfall and has attracted admiring descriptions over many years. One particularly good one from the early 19th century speaks of the 'most remarkable natural object in Brecknockshire' with its 'noble cascade dashing in furious foam ...throwing up clouds of spray and deafening the ear with its complaints'.

This fall, too, was produced by a geological fault, though here the exposed soft shale forms the back wall of the fall and has been eaten away by spraying and dripping water. This has exposed a hard rock platform along which the visitor can safely, if not exactly dryly, walk. It is said that many years ago farmers herded their animals behind the falls in order to cross the Hepste. If true, then that would have been a most remarkable sight. From behind, the falls is extraordinary. Visits to famous places are often anti-climaxes, and this is, after all, only a curtain of water. Rest assured, at Sgwd yr Eira you will not be disappointed.

④ Sgwd y Pannwr

This is the Fuller's Fall, though quite why it should be so named is a mystery. It seems most unlikely that anyone would trek past two perfectly serviceable waterfalls to full his woollen cloth at this one. The most likely explanation is that the foaming base of the short fall reminded the locals of the foam that came off woollen cloth when it was being washed after fulling.

⑤ *The Clun-gwyn Falls*

Sgwd Clun-gwyn means the Fall of the White Meadow. Sgwd Isaf is the Lower Falls and was formed over two parallel fault lines about 150m apart. It is a spectacular fall, the river dropping nearly 30m (90ft) in two leaps, but changing direction as well, the fall line not being at right angles to the river. In addition, the river has eaten back into the pavements of the upper lip to form a tight gorge that prevents easy access to the fall, but increases its scenic appeal.

Sgwd Clun-gwyn, sometimes known as the Upper Clun-gwyn Falls, is an object lesson in waterfall formation. A geological fault has exposed a layer of soft, shaley rock to the river whose bed here is no longer limestone but the less dissolvable sandstone. The shale has been eroded, the river now dropping 10m (30 ft) in two leaps to reach the sandstone again. The fault, in addition to dropping the sandstone block by this distance, also inclined the beds so that the water flows towards the east bank. In wet weather this is barely noticeable, the river filling the shallow horseshoe, but in dry weather the fall is concentrated to the eastern side, to such an extent that it is possible to walk across the sandstone pavement at the western fall edge.

Brecon Beacons

The distinctive flat-topped peaks of the Brecon Beacons – the third mass of Old Red Sandstone, counting from the west, and the one which gives its name to the Park in which it lies – are the most recognisable feature of the Park. For many miles along the Usk valley around Brecon town the peaks of Corn Du and Pen y Fan dominate the southern skyline. As at of Mynydd Ddu, the scarp slopes – and they are very steep indeed – are on the northern and western edges. What is different here is that the ice-sculpting of the scarps has produced a series of marvellous ridges. These ridges, such a feature of walks on the Beacons where they provide more satisfying approaches to the high peaks than on any of the other sandstone masses, enclose equally excellent cwms, their bottoms carved from V-shaped to U-shaped by the passage of ice. Surprisingly there is only one corrie lake, Llyn Cwm-llwch in the cwm formed by ridges running down from the two highest peaks.

To the east the scarp slope runs on much further than the casual visitor realises. The high peaks tend to attract like magnets, leaving a large area, almost half of the mass, largely unpopulated, even on good days. The views from this far end of the scarp are excellent, especially down into the Talybont valley, while the top itself, a narrow plateau produced by the scarp folding back on itself, is interesting for its weird peat deposits.

On the southern side, the Beacons' dip slope is steeper than on the other masses being, almost, a wide valley. This structure has been utilised by the water-gatherers, but offers equally good possibilities for the walker.

WALK 19 | Tommy Jones Memorial Walk

This walk is the 'trade route' up the two highest peaks of the Brecon Beacons and as such should be included in every visitor's itinerary. It also visits two memorials, profoundly different, but equally important in the statement they make. One is a memorial to a young child who died on the hill, the other records the gift of the hill to the people of Britain.

Walk Category: Intermediate/Difficult (3¾ hours) | Length: 9½ km (6 miles) | Ascent: 500m (1600ft) | Maps: Landranger Sheet 160; Outdoor Leisure Sheet 12 | Starting and finishing point: The car-park/layby area beside the A470 Brecon to Merthyr Tydfil road. The car-park is at 988 199, to the east side of the road. There is another (and more obvious) car-park near the Storey Arms Centre, at 983 203, a little way north

At the southern end of the car park a very obvious track leads towards the high peaks, going east through the conifers to reach a kissing gate, then descending to a stream that is crossed by stepping stones. The crossing is distinctly less tricky if there has been a prolonged spell of dry weather. Beyond the stream the made path is difficult to miss as it climbs the hillside (see Note ① of walk 20). Across to the left, walkers can usually be seen on a made path heading up towards Corn Du from the west. The first memorial is reached (see ① National Trust memorial), beyond which the track continues straightforwardly to Bwlch Dwynt, the col between Corn Du, to the left, and an unnamed peak to the right. In its earlier stages the ridge offers fine views to the gorge and the shallow, shelved waterfalls of the Blaen Taf Fawr, while towards the top the long ridge of Craig Cwm-llwch holds the eye.

Looking into Cwm-llwch from the Corn Du/Pen y Fan ridge

Go over Corn Du (see ② Corn Du and Pen y Fan) and climb to the top of Pen y Fan (see, also, Note ②). Retrace your steps to Corn Du, but now go right (north-west) to follow the made path down the beautiful sculpted ridge above Cwm-llwch (see ③ Cwm-llwch). The made path soon bears off left, heading towards the Storey Arms: this is the path observed on the climb which began the walk. We go ahead along the scarred path which continues on the cwm edge, soon reaching the second memorial, (see ④ Tommy Jones memorial). Below the memorial a track leads off right, following the last of the Cwm-llwch ridge cliffs, but we bear left, crossing the hillside to reach the obvious made path which we left higher on the hill. Turn right along this, following it down into the shallow valley of Blaen Taf Fawr cwm to reach a broad col below the shallow hump of Y Gyrn. Cross a stile and continue along the track, descending to the edge of a plantation which is followed to reach a stile. Cross to reach the main A470. Go left, passing the Storey Arms (see ⑤ Storey Arms) to reach the start point car-park.

① *National Trust Memorial*

As the plaque notes, the memorial commemorates the gift of 8,150 acres of the Brecon Beacons to the National Trust by the Eagle Star Insurance Company. This gift, in 1965, has ensured continued access to these fine hills, and will be appreciated by all lovers of the countryside.

② *Corn Du and Pen y Fan*

Corn Du, the Black Horn, and Pen y Fan, the less elegantly named but marginally higher Hill of the Top, are formed of the Upper Series of Old Red Sandstone, from a particular rock type known as Plateau Bed. This is a (relatively)

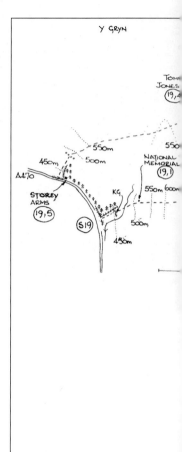

Walks 19 and 20: Brecon Beacons

hard rock whose resistance has resulted in the distinctive 'table-top' structure of the peaks. On top of both peaks, and also on nearby Cribyn, traces of Bronze Age cairns have been found dated to around 1800BC. Little now remains visible to the casual visitor, though when excavated they revealed a number of urns containing ashes from human cremations.

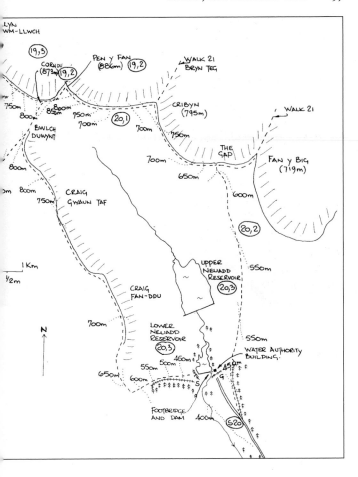

It is thought possible that when the cairns were constructed the high summits of the Brecons supported farming. Today a cooler and wetter climate, and gross overgrazing by sheep, have reduced the land's productivity. From the summit of the two peaks, Cadair Idris and Plynlimon can be seen to the north, while southward Exmoor can be

The Brecon Beacons from the north

picked out across the Bristol Channel.

③ Cwm-llwch

The steep, sculpted edges of Craig Cwm-llwch and Pen y Fan's north-western face make Cwm-llwch a superb example of a glacial cirque. Cirques are formed when originally existing hollows are gradually enlarged either by direct glacial action, or by being snow-filled with consequent frost-erosion. In the case of Cwm-llwch it certainly was glacially hollowed, the glacier-borne debris being deposited near the cwm outflow to form a morainic dam behind which Llyn Cwm-llwch formed when the last Ice Age ended.

④ Tommy Jones Memorial

On 4 August 1900 a Rhondda miner and his five-year old son caught a train to Brecon to visit the miner's parents at their farm in Cwm-llwch. It was getting late as

they began the 6km (4 mile) walk to the farmhouse and by the time they reached Login, a now ruined house then in use as a soldiers' training camp, young Tommy Jones was tired. They rested and were met by Tommy's grandfather and his thirteen-year old cousin Willie. Willie and Tommy set off alone to reach the farmhouse about 800m away, but as dusk fell Tommy was unnerved by the long shadows and started to cry. Willie had been told to alert the farm to the visitors' arrival, and so

he let Tommy return to his father and grandfather alone. The boy had not arrived when Willie rejoined the older men about fifteen minutes later. Within twenty more minutes the Login soldiers were out searching. Next day the police and local folk joined in, but there was no sign of the boy. The search went on for weeks – Tommy's father did not go home for several weeks, and then returned each weekend to search – but without success. The Daily Mail *offered a reward of £20 for* news of Tommy, and tales of kidnap and murder were rife. Finally, in September, a local woman dreamed about the boy, climbed the ridge of Craig Cwm-llwch, which she did not know, and discovered his remains. Tommy had climbed over 400m (1,300ft), and walked at least 3km (2 miles) to reach the remote spot close to where the memorial no stands. The obelisk was erected after a public collection. Mrs Hammer, the lady whose dream had led her to Tommy's body, gave money from the Daily Mail reward she had claimed, and the jury at Tommy's inquest all gave their fees.

The memorial, which was moved a short distance in 1997 when soil erosion threatened to topple it, is a simple, rough-hewn obelisk, a fine tribute. There are many walkers who are unable to pass it without a pause for thought. Tommy's five-year-old legs carried him a long way into very inhospitable country. It is difficult not to be moved by the thought of the boy, desperate to find his father, at first frightened, then panic-stricken as night fell, and finally exhausted. The hills occasionally exact a high price for their wild beauty.

⑤ Storey Arms

Many years before the A470 brought visitors quickly from Brecon to Merthyr Tydfil, a green lane crossed the pass between the Beacons and Forest Fawr. This lane was used by drovers as well as those en route to market, and their thirsts were attended to in the Storey Arms, an inn named after a local family. Later, when the A470 was laid – as a turnpike road and not following the line of the original green lane, the line of which can still be seen on the right bank of the Afon Tarell that drops down to join the Usk at Brecon – the inn became a café. Today it is an outdoor pursuits centre.

WALK 20 | The Neuadd Reservoirs

The long sculpted ridges on the northern face of the Brecon Beacons escarpment naturally attract most of the attention of visitors. The Brecons architecture is not straightforward however, the scarp edge being wrapped around at its eastern and western extremities, and the shallow dip slope being split by a wide valley that holds the two Neuadd reservoirs. Our route takes advantage of this unusual geography, following the scarp edge and visiting the highest tops, but staying on the dip slope throughout its length.

Walk Category: Difficult (5 hours) | Length: 16km (10 miles) | Ascent: 750m (2,450ft) | Maps: Landranger Sheet 160; Outdoor Leisure Sheet 12 | Starting and finishing point: The car-park beside the Blaen Taf Fechan river at 037 170. this is reached from Merthyr Tydfil along the western edge of the Pontsticill and Pentwyn reservoirs. At the northern tip of Pentwyn reservoir, as the road turns sharp right, a lane goes straight on. Follow this lane to the car-park. From the north the same turn is reached by taking a minor road form Talybont-on-Usk – on the B4558 Crickhowell to Brecon road – that goes along the edge of yet another reservoir

From the car-park continue north-westerly towards the obvious mountain wall of the Brecons to reach the building at the tip of the Lower Neuadd reservoir. There is parking available here, but it is ad hoc and can cause access difficulties to the reservoir complex. Our route enters the reservoir compound by way of a gate, turning left to cross the reservoir outlet by footbridge to gain the grassy top of the dam itself. At the end of the dam a gate gives access to open country. Ahead now is a distinct, but thankfully

The Neuadd reservoirs from Pen y Fan

not too eroded path, which heads off towards the corner of the forestry plantation of the left. At the plantation's top corner continue on to reach the ridge. Go right (north) and follow the edges of Craig Fan-ddu and Craig Gwaun Taf to reach the unnamed peak above Bwlch Duwynt. This scarp ridge walk is excellent, the cliffs of Craig Fan-ddu holding the interest until the ridge narrows down to an impressive sharpness, for sandstone country.

From Bwlch Duwynt the peaks Corn Du and Pen y Fan are reached easily (see Notes ② and ③ of Walk 19). The trig point on top of Pen y Fan is set on a real table top, a table that is usually alive with people on good weekend days. To bear witness to the traffic the eastern ridge that we descend, along the top of the impressive cliffs of Craig Cwm Sere, has been badly scarred by countless feet (see ① Path erosion).

From the col at the base of the ridge there is a straightforward and enjoyable walk up Cribyn. This is a fine peak, not quite high enough for a distinctive table top and so a more elegant shape. It is reached, from the north, by the superb ridge of Bryn Teg that is taken by Walk 21. Descend Cribyn's eastern ridge along the edge of Craig Cwm Cynwyn to reach a distinctive pass known as The Gap. If your day is a breezy one there will be a fair wind blowing through The Gap which you will turn into or away from as you turn right (south) onto a broad stony track (see ② Roman road). The track follows the length of the Neuadd reservoirs (see ③ Neuadd reservoirs) towards an obvious forestry plantation. Before this is reached a track goes off right for the ad hoc car-park near the reservoir gate. Ignore this, cross a broad stream gully – a bit of a scramble – to reach the plantation and continue along the track at its edge. This soon reaches the road. Go left to return to the car-park.

① Path erosion

Path erosion is a problem in all of Britain's upland National Parks, a problem caused by the number of people who wish to enjoy the scenery of the Parks at first hand (or, rather, foot!) In the Beacons the problem is exacerbated by the nature of the underlying soil and rock. Unlike parts of North Wales where the rock is hard and the soil thin, here there is an appreciable topsoil though this is washed away as soon as the tramp of many feet has killed off the vegetation – a vegetation kept at minimal length by grazing. The action of washing away the soil causes ruts to form and widen and these become muddy and miserable. The walker, therefore, sadly but not unnaturally, takes to the ground on either side and the process begins again.

Erosion is a problem with no easy solution. If the Park Authorities attempt to stabilise the soil by any of a number of means the artificiality of the techniques is often decried. Yet the only other solution would be an access ban that lasted many years, perhaps even decades, and hard-won access to the hills is unlikely to be relinquished without a contest. Perhaps it is best to recognise that erosion-stabilising programmes are necessary and to be helpful and tolerant of them, and to keep rigidly to the paths and suggested detours.

② Roman Road

There is an old tradition that the track that goes through The Gap, breaching the mountain wall of the Beacons, follows a Roman road. It is certainly true that the Romans had a presence in the area, and that one way of reaching the fort of Cicutium, at 003 297 near Y Gaer about 4km (2½ miles) west of Brecon, would have been to go through The Gap, especially if the intention was to find the most direct way to another fort near Merthyr Tydfil. There is, however, no evidence to support the claim.

③ Neuadd Reservoirs

The lower reservoir, smaller and closer to the start point, was completed in 1884 to supply water to Merthyr

Tydfil, then a boom town of the coal and steel industries. As the industrial expansion continued a second reservoir was required and the upper dam was constructed. The upper reservoir was then, and is now, but only occasionally, known as 'Zulu' for no better reason, apparently, than that its construction coincided with the Zulu Wars!

WALK 21 | Bryn Teg

Walk 19 and 20 explore the best routes to the high peaks of the Brecon Beacons, while Walk 22 below explores the high land at the range's eastern end. That would seem to be enough, but there is one more walk on the Beacons, included for no better reason than that it climbs the best ridge and descends above the best cwm.

Walk Category: Difficult (4½ hours) | Length: 14km (9 miles) | Ascent: 650m (2,130ft) | Maps: Landranger Sheet 160; Outdoor Leisure Sheet 12 | Starting and finishing point: Cantref church, at 056 255 on the road from Llanfrynach that runs west to join the A470 near Libanus. Parking is limited and not easy: please be careful. Alternatives are to use the area at the end of the road beyond Bailea, at 038 237 or at the end of the road beyond Llwyn Fren, at 058 241

From the church (see ① Cantref church) go east, back towards Llanfrynach, taking a track to the right after about 50m. Follow the track to a footbridge over the Afon Cynrig and go diagonally across the field beyond to a stile. Go left and follow the track to a lane. Go right, following the lane past Llwynycelyn Farm to a Y-junction. Either fork can be taken, the right fork over a stream leading to a very sharp left turn for a lane through Neuadd Farm. Bear left at a sharp right turn, walking past Bailea to reach the road end. The left turn reaches Tir-ciw where the metalled lane ends. From there a green lane, difficult in places, leads to a gate and the road end near the entrance to Cwncynwyn Farm.

A stony track now leads south to reach a gate to open country. Ahead is Bryn Teg, one of the most beautiful ridges in Wales. The

The last meters of the Bryn Teg ridge and Cribyn's summit from Pen y Fan

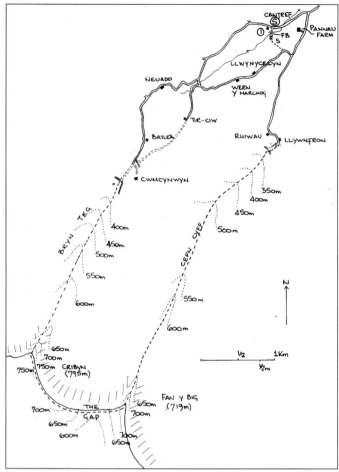

Walk 21: Bryn Teg

translation of the name is Beautiful Hill, so I am not the first to hold this opinion.

Follow Bryn Teg to Cribyn's summit: the last section of the ascent is very steep. At the top, go left (east) to The Gap, following

Walk 20. At The Gap continue eastward, climbing up towards Craig Cwm-oergwm to reach the top of the Cefn Cyff ridge, a point known as Fan y Big, a fine viewpoint. Descend Cefn Cyff, with the magnificent Cwm Oergwm to the right. The ridge descends steeply, flattens out and then falls steeply again. On this last section keep a line of trees to the right and head for a soon obvious gate. Go through this and down the stony track beyond. Soon another gate is reached, beyond which is a metalled lane. Go left on this and follow it for 1.2km (¾ miles) to where a lane goes off left. Take this and after about 250m, as the lane bends left, take the track to the right. This is the outward route which is retraced to the church.

① Cantref Church

The Church of St Mary, Cantref, beautifully set with an approach path through an avenue of fine yew trees, has an early 17th century tower, but much of the rest is new, the nave having been rebuilt and much altered in the 19th century by Charles Buckeridge who was respon-sible for the renovation of several other churches in the area. Inside there is an interesting font, perhaps from as early as the 12th century, though with some overlaying work that suggests that it was reworked at a later time. The churchyard has a number of interesting table tombs and is reached through a delightful, if curious wrought-iron gate.

WALK 22 | The Eastern Beacons

Not surprisingly the high tops of the Beacons, Corn Du and Pen y Fan, attract the majority of visitors. This, together with the fact that The Gap seems to offer a logical eastern end point of the range, means that the huge plateau to the east of The Gap is more rarely visited. In fact this plateau offers fine walking with a distinctly different, almost lunar landscape.

Walk Category: Difficult (4½ hours) | Length: 12km (7½ miles) | Ascent: 550m (1,800ft) | Maps: Landranger Sheet 160; Outdoor Leisure Sheet 12 | Starting and finishing point: The car-park at 056 175 on the minor road from Talybont-on-Usk that is also used to reach the start of Walk 20

From the car-park go back towards the road, crossing the cattle grid or stile, then turning right along a track beside a stream (the Nant Bwrefwr – see Note ③), with the forest to your right. The track leaves the stream, and steepens as it climbs to the top of Craig y Fan Ddu. The path now follows the edge of the scarp as it bears right, then left, then right again. This is a good area for birds, particularly Wheatears, Meadow Pipits and Ravens.

Eventually the long, steep scarp on the right becomes flatter as the head of the Blaen y Glyn is reached, the eye now being drawn to the northern scarp slope which is as long and steep as the one followed earlier. From the scarp edge Brecon can be seen far below. At the valley head a path crosses from right to left. Bear right. There is now a choice as the path forks. Taking the right fork leads towards the outcrop of Cwar y Gigfran and, at 062 200, a memorial as poignant in its way as that to Tommy Jones that we passed on Walk 19 (see ① War memorial). If this route is

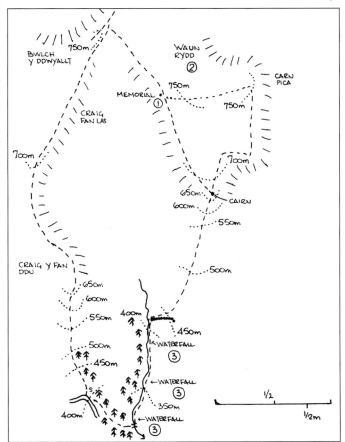

Walk 22: The Eastern Beacons

taken, to continue take a faint, steep path which climbs to the left of the gully above the memorial, turning right when a more distinct path is reached. The path goes above the outcrop of Cwar y Gigfran to reach a prominent cairn.

If the left fork is taken an occasionally indistinct path can be followed across the magnificent, wild peat plateau towards Carn

Pica (see ② Peat hags). Head south from Carn Pica, then follow the scarp edge above Craig y Fan, turning sharp right, then less sharply left above Gwalciau'r Cwm to reach the prominent cairn mentioned above.

From the cairn follow the path heading steeply downhill through a grassy gully to reach a wall. Turn right along this to reach the Blaen Caerfanell. Turn left over a stile and follow a path past several waterfalls (see ③ Waterfalls). When you see a footbridge, cross it and a stile, then turn left into the forest. Soon, take a waymarked right turn and follow the waymarked path steeply uphill through the forest to regain the starting car park.

① War Memorial

The mountains of Wales were a favoured area in World War II for the training of air crews in low-level flying, and as an area where resting crews could keep their hand in. Sadly the Welsh weather took its toll of these crews and several mountains have the remains of planes that came to grief. Perhaps the best-known memorial is that on the summit of Arenig Fawr further to the north, though only because this memorial on the Beacons is off the beaten track. It is to Wellington bomber R1465, a survivor of German raids with 214 Squadron which crashed here in low cloud during a nighttime training exercise on 6 July 1942. The bits of twisted metal are a last reminder of the plane: the Canadian crew of five were all killed, their bodies moved from the plateau for burial.

② Peat Hags

Peat is produced where plant material has been broken down by the processes of decay in a wet environment. In the absence of sufficient oxygen, the normal bacteria and fungi that accelerate decay are absent or limited and instead of rotting away the dead plant material 'humifies' to a jelly-like mass. If this jelly is now pressurised by overlying rocks coal is formed. If there is no overlying material to produce large pressures the jelly instead forms large compact bogs. If the peat is then cut it dries to a stringy dark-brown cake that is useful as a fuel

The eastern Beacons from the Craig Fan-ddu ridge

or to the gardener. Here on the eastern Beacons after the production of a peat bog perhaps 6,000 years ago the climate became drier, and local drainage was aided by early farmers. The peat has therefore dried naturally. In this state it is very easily weathered and ice, frost, wind and rain have created large ruts in the bog. There is no evidence of peat cutting here, so the weathering we see is completely natural. Some of the weathered hags are remarkable: as high as a short walker and weirdly shaped, a bit like surreal mushrooms. As a piece of extraordinary natural architecture it is worth coming many a mile to see.

③ Waterfalls

The largest waterfall, with a drop of 15m (50ft) in total, is a narrow fall, the water landing on an impressive pavement of rock, a by-product of local glaciation. The Nant Bwrefwr's waterfalls are smaller but equally fine. The first, which is split up by numerous jagged columns of rock, is especially good, supporting a fine collection of mosses and other damploving plants.

The Llangattock Escarpment

Immediately east of the Brecon Beacons, indeed connected to it, the walker being able to walk, road-free, from one to the other, is another section of the limestone sheet that once covered the Old Red Sandstones. On the scarp slope above Llangattock the limestone has been quarried and from the Usk valley near Crickhowell the view south is dominated by a line of low, vertical cliffs that contour around the hill just below the skyline. The limestone is carboniferous, and the quarrymen broke into numerous caves which have been explored to yield one of Britain's most significant caving areas. On top of the quarried cliffs there are frequent pools in the plateau. It is an odd discovery, indeed totally unexpected: how can water lie in small pools when only yards away it has dissolved its way into the rock to form extensive caves? The answer is straightforward. Just south of the cliffs the limestone sheet had itself been overlain with a sheet of impervious Millstone Grit. This harder, less easily weathered rock forms a poor soil and the area of Mynydd Llangattock and Mynydd Llangynidr is boggy country with little vegetation apart from stiff ling. It is a wild, vaguely hostile country, offering fine uncompromising walking.

WALK 23 | Chartists' Cave

The plateau-like land beyond the escarpment that sits above the Usk valley is split into two halves by a road across it from Beaufort, near Brynmawr, to Llangynidr. Each half offers a fine, if rugged, walk on rarely visited moorland. Our first walk takes the western half, visiting a cave that probably had historical significance. This walk is not for the inexperienced if the weather is poor. Good visibility is required unless it is to be followed solely by use of a compass or GPS – a procedure which rather defeats the object, even if it is good practice – and it is better not to tackle the walk after continuous heavy rain which can make the going arduous and very wet.

Walk Category: Intermediate/Difficult (3 hours) | Length: 11km (7 miles) | Ascent: 250m (800ft) | Maps: Landranger Sheet 161; Outdoor Leisure Sheet 13 | Starting and finishing point: At 160 164 on the minor road from Beaufort, near Brynmawr, to Llangynidr, on the B4558 Crickhowell to Brecon 'back road'. This plateau-crossing minor road is unfenced and studded with parking spaces. That suggested is close to the quarry at 159 163 which is the first objective of the walk

Take the track to the old stone quarry – care is needed in the quarry itself as there is an unprotected pot-hole in its floor – and climb out of its back by going to the left of the cave. From the top an indistinct track leads off southward – on a bearing of 205° – passing a spectacular series of swallet or shake holes (see Note ② of Walk 18) many 15-20m (50-60ft) deep. Please be careful, the holes are not all well protected and their edges can be unstable.

From the top of the small rise ahead the Llangynidr reservoir can be seen – if the weather is clear – and this gives the line. The

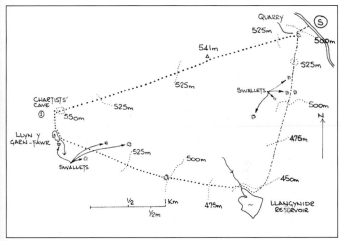

Walk 23: Chartists' Cave

reservoir is fenced, so follow the fence westward towards the reservoir tip where an inflowing stream is crossed. Westward now, on a bearing of 275°, there is a large pile of stones on the skyline. Head for this and continue past it on the same bearing, heading for the small lake of Llyn y Garn-fawr at 126 149. In dry weather – when the walk is at its easiest – this lake can dry up completely, but there is a large pile of stones at its southern end which gives the line in clear weather.

From the lake's northern tip Chartists' Cave is a mere 300m away on a bearing of 30°, but do not be deceived, the cave can be very difficult to find. From the cave (see ① Chartists' Cave) the return journey is more straightforward – on a clear day. On a bearing of 75° the trig point at 147 159 is visible and is the next objective. There are indistinct tracks in this area, but nothing is really better than a direct route across the moor. From the trig

The Brecon Beacons from near Chartists' Cave

point the quarry is on a bearing of 77°, though things become easier the closer the walker is to it.

① Chartist's Cave

The Poor Law of 1834 caused great resentment among poor working people throughout Britain because its implication was not only that the poor were responsible for their poverty, but that they should be made to suffer for it. The resentment was seen in the growth of unionism, and also in the birth of Chartism. Chartists were those who supported the People's Charter of 1838, a six-point charter calling for full male suffrage, secret ballots, and the abolition of property qualifications

for Members of Parliament. Today
the requests seem reasonable enough,
but the threat they posed to the established order in 1838 was enormous.
The local Chartists' leader in South
Wales was John Frost, a strong-
willed man of fifty-five. In late
1839 Frost was convinced that
Chartists all over the country were
about to rise up and seize power, and
so he organised an armed uprising to
take Newport, then the region's
largest town. Legend has it that Frost
and the other leaders stayed in the
cave here during the last days before
the march, and that other caves in
the Llangattock escarpment held men
making weapons. Other versions of
the story suggest that the caves held
weapons, but not necessarily men,
and it is this version which appears
on the plaque which was attached

above the cave's entrance in 1989 to celebrate the 150th anniversary of the uprising.

Frost had hoped that 50,000 men would follow him to Newport, but in the event on a cold and miserably wet November day there were a great deal fewer. How many exactly is open to conjecture. Frost maintained there were only 400, though the Mayor of Newport claimed that there were 20,000. As each side had a vested interest in exaggeration it is likely that the real figure was about 5,000, most of them armed, if at all, only with pitchforks.

The Chartists marched to the Westgate Hotel and were met there by the Mayor and a squadron of soldiers. Words were exchanged and then a shot was fired. Later each side blamed the other for the shot, but that is academic now. The soldiers opened fire killing around twenty of the men. Frost was arrested – the 'rebellion' was over. At his trial Frost, together with several others, was sentenced to death, but recognition that this would create martyrs meant that the sentences were commuted to transportation for life to Tasmania. In fact Frost served fifteen years, returning to Britain to live to the ripe old age of ninety-three and remaining strong-willed to the last.

WALK 24 | The Llangattock Quarries

This walk takes the eastern half of the high plateau above the Usk Valley. In its early stages it is well-defined, following an old tramway past some good industrial relics, a unique nature reserve and the entrances to some fine caves. Thereafter it ascends the plateau to visit a mysterious lake. As with the last walk the plateau is no place to be if the weather is poor, the more so in this case as the cliffs of the old quarries start abruptly and are both vertical and high.

Walk Category: Intermediate/Difficult (2½ hours) | Length: 10km (6 miles) | Ascent: 200m (650ft) | Maps: Landranger Sheet 161; Outdoor Leisure Sheet 13 | Starting and finishing point: From Brynmawr a mountain road runs around the Llangattock escarpment before dropping down into Llangattock village and continuing to Crickhowell. The road is a fine outing in itself: at the Brynmawr end there are magnificent views out over the Usk Valley and the Black Mountains, while the drop is a first-class test of driving skills, being both steep and narrow – and occasionally both together – and having unyielding walls on both sides. On this road, at 209 155 there is an obvious stony track going up towards the quarries. Park at any convenient place near the bottom of this. There are more places on the Brynmawr side (the eastern side) of the incline. Please park tidily

From your parking place return of the bottom of the track and take it to a ruined building near its top. This is the ruin of an old limekiln, and dates from the time when the quarries were in full production (see ① Llangattock Quarries). Behind the ruin is the Darren Quarry, but we do not visit it, going, instead, to the right on a rough track, sometimes grassy, sometimes stony, along which

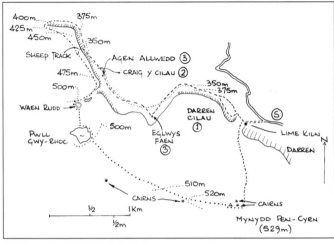

Walk 24: The Llangattock Quarries

once ran a quarry tramway. To the left, just after leaving the building, there is a break in the otherwise continuous quarry wall. The return route uses this break to drop through the cliffs.

The old tramway veers off to the Pant-y-Rhiw Quarry and although it is possible to take a direct line, to the right of the now grassy spoil cones, it is worth visiting the quarry itself. It is popular with outdoor centres and there are frequently trainee rock climbers at work on its walls. At the left (east) end is a small pond that is favoured by dragonflies, while at its right (west) end the line of cliffs is almost breached by the debris of a massive rock fall that occurred in the late 1940s. Near this landslip, and more especially in the continuation of the quarry beyond, there are superb flowstone formations on the upper quarry walls.

Beyond the formidable wall of the continuation quarry, the cliff wall is more broken. This is Craig y Cilau, a National Nature Reserve (see ② Craig y Cilau). Beneath the cliffs the old tramway appears again, offering a straightforward way of reaching, at 193

155, the huge entrance of Eglwys Faen, one of the numerous caves that are found in the escarpment (see ③ Quarry caves). Another cave entrance, to Agen Allwedd (see ③ is reached at 188 158. In contrast to the easily accessible Eglwys Faen, the entrance here is gated to prevent inexperienced explorers from gaining access to one of Britain's longest cave system. Beyond Agen Allwedd the tramway ends, though progress is still possible along the cliff base. To gain the top of the cliffs it is necessary to continue to the clear cliff left-turn at 183 167 and then for another 500m to where the fading cliffs give way to steep, but easily climbed, slopes. An alternative to this extension is to take an obvious, but exposed, route up the steep track just beyond Agen Allwedd. This track is clear enough but can be dangerous if wet or icy. If using it, please take great care.

Whether the long route or the steep track is taken, the walker should walk back (eastwards) along the cliff edge until a steep gully blocking progress is reached. Now head south-west – along the line of the gully – to reach a small pool, often dry in summer, and the impressive swallet or shake hole of Waen Rudd (see Note ② of Walk 18). Those used to the swallets of Walk 23 will be stunned by the sheer size of Waen Rudd. Water that sinks here reappears in the entrance series of Agen Allwedd.

From Waen Rudd go due south across the moor to reach Pwll Gwy-rhoc, a brown lake that seems to lurk among the heather. Though I have used the now prevalent spelling I am inclined to believe that it is a fanciful rendering of Gwrhoc, Welsh for witch, a name that seems entirely appropriate for this vaguely mysterious body of water.

From the pool, head south-east to the obvious high ground and follow a shallow ridge, topped by several Bronze Age cairns, to the trig point summit of Mynydd Pen-Cyrn. From the summit go east to reach an indistinct track that heads northward to reach the safe descent through the line of quarry cliffs that we noted on the outward route. Now follow the outward route back to the start.

① Llangattock Quarries

The taking of stone from the Llangattock escarpment probably began in earliest times, the stone being readily available as the steep slope produced rock outcrops. It was not until the early 19th century, however, that the commercial exploitation of the escarpment started. The opening of the Brecon and Abergavenny Canal – followed by Walk 31 – gave quarrymen easy access to markets, and a tramway was built from the quarries to Llangattock Wharf. In all, three inclines were built, each powered by gravity, i.e. full trolleys going down to the wharf pulled a number of empty trolleys up the incline.

It was not stone that was the chief export, but lime, used for 'sweetening' agricultural land. Most of the lime was produced by burning the stone at the wharf, a fairly logical procedure as coal could be unloaded from the canal barges directly into the kilns. Later however a kiln was constructed at the Darren Quarry. Presumably it was calculated that hauling coal up the incline was worth the effort, the downward-travelling trolleys being able to carry far more finished lime than raw stone.

By the 1830s the need for lime for agriculture had become secondary, the growth of the iron industry in South Wales now requiring vast quantities of limestone as a furnace flux. The quarries at Llangattock were extended, new tramways were built and the area became very prosperous. The boom was relatively short-lived: within fifty years more efficient ways of making steel reduced the need for limestone. The need for agricultural lime kept the quarries active at a reduced level, but by the early years of the 20th century even that requirement was decreasing. In 1920 the last shipment of stone was burnt at Llangattock Wharf and, soon after, the quarries were silent.

Today the escarpment is a fascinating place for the industrial archaeologist. There are old buildings, old inclines and tramways – now mainly grassed over, but their tracks still visible – spoil heaps and even the odd rarity: just below the tramway as it nears Pant-y-Rhiw Quarry a rusting pair of lines disappear into a tight horizontal mine shaft. But the site is also a dangerous one and extreme caution should be exercised by anyone intending to explore the buildings, caves and shafts.

Craig y Cilau

② Craig y Cilau

The English translation of the Welsh is Refuge Crag which is entirely apt, if fortuitous. The cliffs here are steep enough to prevent sheep grazing, but not vertical, so that a quite remarkable plant culture has survived. Alpine Enchanter's Nightshade is at its British southern limit on the cliffs, and here too are the angular Solomon's Seal, Thistle Broomrape and Maiden Pink. But the chief delights are the trees. There is a small beech wood – one of Europe's most westerly stands – lime, both large and small-leaved, and yew. There are also six species of sorbus, the fairly common Rowan (Mountain Ash) and five rare varieties. Two of these are known only in this part of Wales, while one, Sorbus minima, is virtually confined to this area. The tree, a lesser whitebeam, was 'discovered' in the late 19th century by the Revd Augustine Ley, and was believed to have become extinct when a large rock-fall destroyed all known specimens about fifty years ago. Thankfully a few specimens did survive, and there are now several trees on the cliff.

In 1959 the special nature of Craig y Cilau was recognised when the site – a total of 157 acres – was made a National Nature Reserve. There is unrestricted access for the public, and it goes without saying that every care should be taken to avoid damage not only to the trees, shrubs and plants, but to the cliffs themselves. The collecting of plants is forbidden without the permission of the Nature Conservancy.

③ *Quarry Caves*

The limestone of the Llangattock escarpment is carboniferous, the form that dissolves readily in acidic water. Not surprisingly then there are caves here, many of which have been broken into by the quarrying operations. The cave systems are so extensive that Llangattock is now one of the most important caving centres in Britain. Ogof-y-Darren Cilau, at 206 153 behind the ruined limekiln at the start of the walk, starts with a long, tight, wet crawl of the type that makes cavers purr with delight and gives non-cavers the heebie-jeebies at the very thought. The cave is now explored for over 6km (4 miles). Eglwys Faen – the Stone Church –

which our walk passes is, by contrast, only about 1km (1,100 yards) long. The huge entrance beside the tramway is one of several into the cave and leads directly to the vast chamber that gives the cave its name. The casual visitor can penetrate some distance into the chamber guided by light streaming in through the entrance, but do take care: the ground is uneven and boulder-strewn. Elsewhere the cave has an aven, an upper passage, reached by one member of the party ascending a vertical squeeze in order to let down a ladder through a hole in the roof for other members to climb.

Agen Allwedd, whose gated entrance we also pass, is the largest local system at almost 35km (over 20 miles). At one time Aggie, as it is known in caving circles, was the longest cave in Wales, but is has long since lost that title to Ogof Ffynnon Ddu cave near the start of Walk 15. The cave's name means Keyhole Cleft, a reference to its original entrance that was shaped like a keyhole. The cave has one chamber large enough to house St Paul's Cathedral, reached by a passage so tight that it can only be negotiated with perseverance and difficulty.

The Black Mountains

The last, the easternmost, block of Old Red Sandstone is a fine mass with a northern scarp slope as elsewhere, but a long, shallow dip slope ending more steeply, with a drop into the Usk valley. The Sandstone block has also been river-carved and a series of essentially north-south valleys has been formed. The effect of this has been to produce a hand-like structure with a series of finger ridges pointing south, these joined across the northern scarp edge. To the east is a ridge above the Vale of Ewyas, a ridge taken by the Offa's Dyke National Trail, terminating at Hay Bluff. The Vale of Ewyas carries a road that crosses the northern scarp, by way of Gospel Pass, its western side being formed by a ridge that divides Ewyas from the Grwyne Fawr valley. Next are two ridges joined at Waun Fach, the highest summit on the mass, that define the valley of the Grwyne Fechan river that flows past Llanbedr. West of the ridge from Waun Fach to Pen Cerrig-calch is the valley of the Rhian-goll taken by the A479. This valley's western side is defined by the Black Mountains' most westerly ridge.

The well-defined and low-lying valleys give the Black Mountains a gentle pastoral feel, a contrast to the upland moor of the defining ridges.

WALK 25 | Mynydd Troed

Those who have travelled on the A479 from Talgarth to Crickhowell will know that as they twist and turn upwards out of Talgarth they have before them one of the most perfect ridges in Wales, an apparent knife edge to a conical peak. Things are not as they seem, as we shall see, but the ridge of Mynydd Troed does offer a superb walk, and is short enough to use as a gentle introduction to the hill-walking of the Brecon Beacons National Park.

Walk Category: Easy (2½ hours) | Length: 8km (5 miles), though shorter if the full ridge is not walked | Ascent: 350m (1,150ft) | Maps: Landranger Sheet 161; Outdoor Leisure Sheet 13 | Starting and finishing point: Almost at the top of the pass that the A479 from Talgarth to Crickhowell takes to cross the Black Mountains there is a telephone box on the east side. Beside this is a lay-by with parking for several cars

From the lay-by go south, i.e. towards Crickhowell, and take the first lane on the right-hand (west) side, after about 150m. Follow this, going through a gated compound, to open country. Here the path goes ahead – we take it on our return journey – but we go left to tackle the ridge of Mynydd Troed. Sadly the ridge turns out to be much broader than it looks and leads to a summit that is, in fact, only the high end point of a long north-south running ridge. Nevertheless the walk is a fine one and the summit is a fine vantage point (see ① Mynydd Troed). To get full benefit from the peak's position it is best to walk south along the ridge. A full-length walk – to the point at which the gently sloping ridge falls much more steeply – involves a round trip of about 3km (2 miles) and an ascent of 60m (200ft) on the return leg. The walk can therefore be shortened by that amount if the ridge is not traversed.

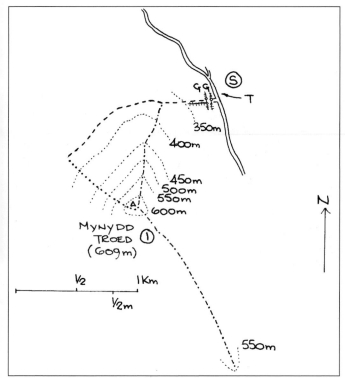

Walk 25: Mynydd Troed

To descend go south of the trig point to reach a path that descends the west flank of the hill to reach the path that we left on the outward journey. Go right and follow it back to the start.

① *Mynydd Troed*

The importance of the uplands of Wales to the Celts is detected in the number of words they had to describe meadows and hills, each one unique in its description of the countryside and its usefulness for agriculture or defence. For hills there are pen, twyn, carnedd *and* moch *– to*

Mynydd Troed

name only the major ones – each with a fairly indifferent translation into English. The peak here is a mynydd, *usually translated as a mountain, which is a rather grand title for an elongated grassy ridge that just fails to reach the 2,000ft contour.* Troed *means leg or foot and could (just) refer to the shapely elegance of the ridge when seen from the Talgarth side.*

From the peak the view of the Rhian-goll valley and the far wall of the Black Mountains is superb, perhaps the best from any vantage point on the range – though that on

Walk 29 is also a front runner – while the view northward over the Wye valley and the Welsh Marches is equally good. Eastward the position of the peak, at the western extremity of the range, means that there are extensive views over pleasant farmland. Llyn Syfaddan, or Llangorse Lake as it is more usually known, is also visible. This is the largest natural lake in South Wales and a place of legend. One local tale is of a village that stood where the lake now is, but was swallowed by an earthquake and now rests below the water. When the water is rough the old church bell can be heard chiming and an old woman from the village occasionally surfaces to kidnap a child. The latter part of the tale of the Old Woman of the Lake has, apparently, been used to frighten the local kids with a slight change to her behaviour, so that she only kidnaps disobedient children! Interestingly it is now known that there was once a village on the crannog, a man-made island, that lies close to the lake's northern shore. It was almost certainly a Celtic village and the dating of a dug-out canoe found at the site suggests that it could have been inhabited as late as AD800. Could it be that a folk memory of a village on the crannog gave rise to the legend of the submerged village?

Gerald of Wales mentioned the lake and as a good lover of legends noted that it occasionally turned bright green and was also occasionally streaked blood-red. In winter, he said, it moo-ed like a herd of cows. It is probable that each of these stories has a basis in truth, the colour changes being algal 'blooms', the noise being ice cracking. More likely to be a real legend is his story that the birds of the lake will sing only for the rightful king of Wales.

As a natural lake Llangorse – which Gerald called Brecknock Mere or Clamosus – has a superb collection f water plants, fish and birds. The fish were famous for their immense size, the local expression for conveying hugeness being cyhyd a llyswen syfaddan, as long as a Syfaddan eel. Sadly 'has' is almost becoming 'had', as the lake has no protection as a national site and is a centre for all sorts of water sports which interfere with the birds and destroy the vegetation. With so many artificial sheets of water in South Wales it is a shame that Llangorse could not have been left alone.

WALK 26 | Waun Fach

The elongated ridges of the Black Mountains make circular walks difficult, and horseshoe walks – taking the line of the northern scarp slope to link ridges – long. The very best walk is to start at Llanbedr (see Walk 27) and to take the Crug Mawr ridge to Waun Fach, returning over Table Mountain. That is a very long trip and outside the scope of this book. Instead we shall explore that same country in two walks. That idea has the distinct advantage, the ascent of one of the most delightful ridges in South Wales.

On the A479 from Talgarth to Crickhowell it is the sharp ridge of Mynydd Troed (Walk 25) that takes the eye. If instead the travellers is going north, from Crickhowell to Talgarth, the eye is drawn to a peaked ridge that leads west-east as a buttress to the long north-south Black Mountains ridge. Our walk takes that ridge, and visits the highest peaks of the Black Mountains range.

Walk Category: Difficult (5 hours) | Length: 16km (10 miles) | Ascent: 750m (2,450ft) | Maps: Landranger Sheet 161; Outdoor Leisure Sheet 13 | Starting and finishing point: At 175 295, the car park on the left (east) side of the A479 just a short distance south of the start of Walk 25, close to the Castle Inn

Go down the steps at the rear of the car park, turning right at the bottom, then left over a stile. Follow the permissive path beyond, crossing a stream and another stile. Follow the left edge of the field beyond, climbing to a stile which gives access to Castell Dinas (see ① Castell Dinas). Go over the castle site, bearing left, then right to descend steeply on to a track. Cross this and continue ahead, climbing the first section (to Y Grib) of the fine 'skyline' ridge to Pen y Manllwyn.

The start of the beautiful ridge to Pen y Manllwyn

Pen y Manllwyn is not a real peak, just the last hump on a broad ridge that falls northward from Waun Fach. Go right (south-east) and follow the ridge to the summit of Waun Fach (see ② Waun Fach and Pen y Gadair Fawr). From the summit, more a broad plateau than a top, the huge cairn on top of Pen y Gadair Fawr is visible to the south-east. To reach it and return means an out-and-back walk over rough country, but who could resist such a summit?

From Pen y Gadair Fawr (see, also, Note ②) return to Waun Fach. Now head south of west on a path along the narrowing ridge of Pen Trumau. Follow the path as it steepens down the peak's southern spur. At the broad col between Pen Trumau and Mynydd Llysiau ahead, turn right along a clear track which descends, increasingly steeply, to reach a gate. Follow the walled track beyond to a road. Turn right, then first left on a road which

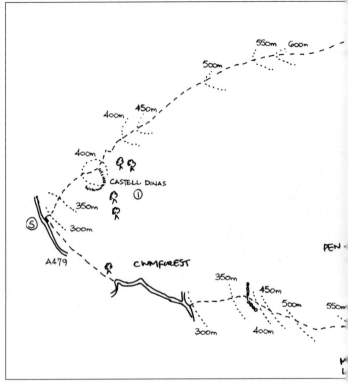

Walk 26: Waun Fach

descends, then rises again. Now, as the road turns very sharply left, turn right along a farm track which leads back to the steps used on the outward route.

① Castell Dinas

The Castell Dinas hill fort stands on a final detached knob of the Y Grib ridge that our walk follows. It is, like most hill forts, Iron Age. Iron Age forts went through a succession of clearly defined steps in the evolution of their defences. At first the natural defences might be augmented by a

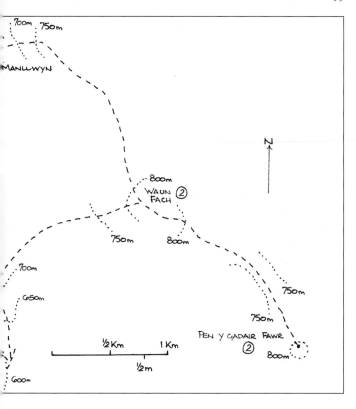

ditch and rampart, but later, when the attackers were armed with sling shots, there was a need to keep them further back and more ditches and ramparts were required. Here at Castell Dinas two huge ramparts were constructed at points where the naturally defensive steepness of the spur needed reinforcing. The fort's gate was at the north-ern end, though there is evidence of a second gate at the south-east.

A thousand years after the earliest occupation the Normans needed to hold the Rhian-goll valley in order to control access to the Usk valley their main thoroughfare in this part of Wales. At first they constructed a motte within the ramparts of Castell

Summit cairn, Pen y Gadair Fawr

Dinas, before moving down the valley
to Tretower.

② *Waun Fach and Pen y Gadair Fawr*

The summit of Waun Fach, the
Little Moor, cannot readily be called
the high spot of the Black Mountains,
even if it is the highest spot. The
actual top is marked by a thick, circular trig point base set among a
morass of churned-up peat.

    Pen y Gadair Fawr is more
sharply defined and therefore better

drained peak. Its summit cairn is a
wonder of the cairn builder's art and
is a good place to take in the view.
To the east the valley of the Grwyne
Fechan is heavily afforested – though
the visitor to it will find it a delightful mix of hard and soft woods at
stream level – and finishes with a
small reservoir. The Llanbedr valley
to the west is more pastoral. From
Waun Fach the distinctive cone of
Sugar Loaf can be seen, and there is
a fine view along the continuous
scarp line to the north.

WALK 27 | Table Mountain

This is the second of the walks that explore the finest of the Black Mountains' ridges. It also has the advantage of visiting Table Mountain, the curious truncated peak that dominates the view of the range from Crickhowell and other nearby spots in the Usk valley.

Walk Category: Difficult (5 hours) | Length: 18km (11¼ miles) | Ascent: 680m (2,250ft) | Maps: Landranger Sheet 161; Outdoor Leisure Sheet 13 | Starting and finishing point: The village of Llanbedr, reached by minor roads from Crickhowell or Glangrwyne on the A40 Abergavenny to Brecon road. Beside the village church there is room for a small number of cars. Please park carefully and tidily

From the church (see ① Llanbedr) take the lane going north beside the public house to a T-junction of lanes. There go right and follow the lane for about 2km (1½ miles) to where it doubles back on itself as it crosses a stream. There is a car park on the left here which can be used as an alternative start. Go over a stile at the back of the car park and bear half-right, uphill to a waymarker post. Go along the field edge to reach a stile. Go over and half-right to reach a path junction. Turn half-left on the sunken track, following it to a stile beyond which a rough track leads uphill to a stile near the corner of a plantation. Beyond, follow the forest edge towards a prominent cairn. Continue along a path which heads up the broad spur ahead. The spur forms the eastern edge of Cwm Banw, and after visiting the top of Pentwynglas where our spur ends, we follow the broad main ridge around the head of Cwm Banw. The main ridge here is flat as well as broad, but it rears up steeply to reach the summit of Pen Allt-mawr.

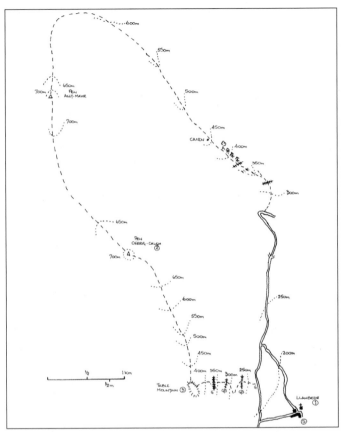

Walk 27: Table Mountain

Ahead the ridge is again broad, though now it gently descends as we follow it southward. About 1km (½ mile) south of Pen Allt-mawr it splits into two broad ridges. The rightward one – Pen Gloch-y-Pibwr – is only a spur and rapidly ends in a descent to the Rhian-goll valley. Our walk takes the left ridge, which heads south-east and down to the shallow peak of Pen Cerrig-calch (see ② Pen Cerrig-calch).

From the summit of Pen Cerrig-calch a path heads off south-east towards the as-yet unseen Table Mountain. When that peak does at last come into view, it is a bit disappointing as it is nothing like as eye-catching as it appears from the valleys. The peak (see ③ Table Mountain) itself is an interesting place being much more tilted than is apparent from below, and offering superb views of the Usk valley. To continue go east – most walkers will actually exit from the hill fort on the peak by going back northward and then make their way around to the east side – to reach a path that goes down through a gate to reach a gate and stile. Beyond is a track that is followed past another gate and stile to the road. Go right, taking the first lane to the left and following that back to Llanbedr.

① Llanbedr

The earliest church at the village was consecrated in 1060 and it is believed that part of this still exists as the nave, though that was widened in the 16th century. The tower is older, being a 14th-century addition to the original building and con-structed at a time when the Normans were keen on building towers as much as places of refuge as to satisfy more spiritual needs. Inside, the church has some interesting pieces while outside the lych gate and the yew trees are excellent.

Going in the opposite direction from our Walk the visitor will reach a superb pack-horse bridge over the Grwyne Fechan river. The bridge has not been precisely dated, but is certainly medieval.

② Pen Cerrig-calch

From the Usk valley, on sunny days, a patch of white sparkles on the top of Pen Cerrig-calch making many visitors wonder, especially in winter, whether there is snow on the peak. The walker will find that what sparkles is not snow, but limestone. The Old Red Sandstone that is such a feature of the Black Mountains – as well as of the other hills of the National Park – was laid down in the Devonian era of geological time which ended about 345 million years ago. Following that, sheets of lime-stone were laid down during the

Pen Allt-mawr, left, Waun Fach, centre, and Pen y Gadair Fawr from the limestone plateau of Pen Cerrig-calch

Carboniferous period. These were overlain by Millstone Grit before the period ended about 280 million years ago. The tilt of the land allowed weathering to begin early on the northern slopes so that whereas on Walk 24 we saw limestone with its quarries and caves and visited a pool on impermeable Millstone Grit, on walks on the Black Mountains the walker expects to find only the Old Red Sandstone, the younger

rocks having completely weathered away. Pen Cerrig-calch has a few remaining feet of the original overlying limestone sheet still intact.

The peak's name is interesting. It means Peak of the Limestone Rocks and indicates that the early Welsh farmers, though they might not have understood the geological processes that gave rise to the white rock sheet, certainly understood their area well enough to recognise its existence.

③ *Table Mountain*

Table Mountain is a typical hill fort in a wonderfully defensive position with commanding views over the Usk valley. As with Castell Dinas (see Note ① of Walk 26) the natural defences of the site have been supplemented by ramparts. On all sides — if sides is the right descriptive word for a fort that is essentially circular — there are two ramparts,

while in the obviously weaker areas the number has been increased to four. The Welsh name for the peak, more properly for the fort itself, is Crug Hywel, Hywel's Fort. By tradition the Hywel of the name is Hywel Dda. Hywel the Good. Hywel was a Welsh king of the 10th century, so strictly the fort pre-dates him by a thousand years, but the site is so obviously excellent strategically that there is no reason to believe that

The medieval bridge at Crickhowell and, beyond, Table Mountain and Pen Cerrig-calch

a later Welsh king operating before the age of castles would not have occupied the site.

Hywel was an interesting man. He is usually stated to have been the first Welsh king to have united Wales into one kingdom, though that he did not do, for although he ruled Gwynedd, Powys and Dyfed he failed to secure Gwent and Glamorgan. He is termed 'the Good' for his codification of Welsh law which gave certain legal rights to his subjects. As an example, the laws gave women equal property rights with men, a very forward-looking piece of legislation. The laws also laid down certain requirements and definitions which meant that the common man was not forever at the mercy of landowners and merchants. Some of the definitions are eccentric, but great fun. A good mouser cat was worth a sheep, and gold plate must be 'as thick as the nail of a ploughman who has been a ploughman for seven years'. Hywel also laid down the duties of some of the royal household for the first time. These are also interesting, and equally good fun. There was even a Royal Footholder who sat under the king's table ready to scratch the royal foot when required!

Crug Hywel has given its name to Crickhowell, the fine town on the Usk that stands at the base of the peak. When the Normans came they placed their castle there rather than on the peak and its remains can still be visited. The castle was built by a governor with the unlikely name of Sir Grimbaud Pauncefoot. Perhaps in deference to the difficulties (or mirth) of this name, the castle is known as Alisby's Castle after a later owner. While in the town do visit the Usk Bridge a fine early 18th-century construction with twelve arches on one side and thirteen on the other. Just outside Crickhowell at Gwernvale, in a building that is now a hotel, Sir George Everest after whom the world's highest mountain is named, was born.

WALK 28 | The Grwyne Fawr Valley

On the eastern side the Black Mountains' ridges define two ribbon-like valleys. The wider of these is the more easterly, the one taken by Walk 29. The valley of the Grwyne Fawr is tighter. In its upper reaches it is heavily forested and although the stream flows through some very pretty mixed moorland – and is the haunt of the Dipper, that most delightful of water birds – the walking is short or too often lost in the trees. Where the trees end, however, there is a delightful stretch of valley, and a fine walk links the two eastern valleys, a small hamlet, a rare and fascinating old church and a stone linked to an old Welsh legend.

Walk Category: Intermediate (4½ hours) | Length: 12km (7½ miles) | Ascent: 500m (1,650ft) | Maps: Landranger Sheet 161; Outdoor Leisure Sheet 13 | Starting and finishing point: The village of Cwmyoy reached from the road that runs from Llanvihangel Crucorney – on the A465 north of Abergavenny – to Hay-on-Wye by way of the Afon Honddu's valley, known as the Vale of Ewyas, and Gospel Pass. There is very limited car-parking below the church. Please park carefully and tidily

From the church (see ① Cwmyoy) follow the village road down past Cwmyoy Farm to reach a signed footpath at the second gate to the right. Go across the field with the fence on your right hand to a footbridge over the Afon Honddu. Go up, crossing a stile to reach the road. Go over the road and up the lane to Coed Farm, going through the farm and up left into the forest. Cross a forest road, continuing left and uphill to reach the forest edge. Here go

Approaching Partrishow Church

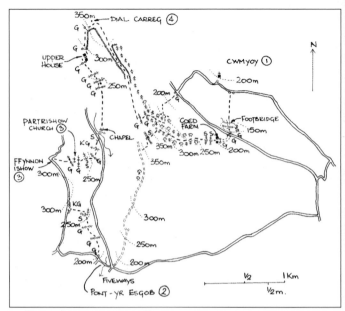

Walk 28: The Grwyne Fawr Valley

across a field to a wall and over it, by a stile, on to an open ridge. Go left, following the wall for about 100m to reach a track going right. Follow this to a lane. Turn left on this and follow it all the way to the bottom of the Grwyne Fawr valley at Five-Ways, a noted local landmark.

Take the Crickhowell road, the one going west, and cross Pont-yr-Esgob (see ② Pont-yr-Esgob). Go up to a Y-junction and there go through the gate to the right. Follow a track across two fields to a gate near a ruined farmhouse. Turn half-right and cross the field, turning left at its boundary hedge to follow the hedge to a lane. Go right along the lane, following it to a sharp right-hand bend. To the right here is Ffynnon Ishow (see ③ Partrishow church), set back a little from the road. Go around the sharp bend to reach the path for Partrishow church (see, also, Note ③).

After spending time in the church – and Partrishow church is worth all the time you can spare – continue through the church-yard to reach a path which is followed down to Ty'n-y-llwyn Farm. Go through the farm and down a track to the road. Go left, then, after about 70m, right to a bridge over the Grwyne Fawr river. Take the left fork at a Y-junction, going past the Tabernacle Chapel, and follow the lane past two farms, Ty-mawr and Upper House to a gate on to the hillside. Go through and follow the wall, right, to the Dial Carreg memorial (see ④ Dial Carreg).

Continue on the obvious track past Dial Carreg to where a zig-zag path goes ahead, dropping down into the Honddu valley. That path can be followed, but a more satisfactory route is to bear right with the track (which eventually leads to the outward route). Before it is reached, however, a gate left gives access to the forest. Go along the track to reach a forest road. Here go left and almost immediately right on another track. Leave the track to go left on next path, following it to a fence and stile. Go over and turn half-right, going downhill across the field to a gate on to a lane. Go left, then right after 50m on a lane back to Cwmyoy.

---

① *Cwmyoy*

Cwmyoy means the Valley – or, more correctly, the Cwm, that is a valley with a headwall – of the Yoke. With a little imagination it is possible to see that the valley is yoke-shaped, though it is nowhere near as obvious as the name would imply. The Church of St Martin is medieval and is curious in having not one square in its construction. This seems more likely to be because of the shape of the bed rock, and its occa-sional subsidence, than because of incompetent builders. The medieval cross in the church has a curious his-tory. It was discovered at a local farm in the late 19th century but disappeared from the church tower in 1967. A photograph of it was shown to the Keeper of Statuary at the British Museum, who dated it to the 13th century and remembered that he had recently seen it in a near-by antiques shop. The cross was repossessed and brought back to Cwmyoy.

② Pont-yr-Esgob

On the first series of the Ordnance Survey's Outdoor Leisure Sheet to the Black Mountains the bridge or, more correctly, the house near it is marked as Pontysbig. On the newest series the name is rendered as Pontyspig. On both sheets a nearby mill was marked as Pont Esgob. Each of these is a misrepresentation, the last a near-miss at least, of Pont-yr-Esgob, the Bishop's bridge.

The bridge is name for Archbishop Baldwin, the travelling companion of Gerald of Wales. In truth, of course, the reverse is true since Gerald, a Welsh Norman born at Manorbier Castle in Pembrokeshire, was Archdeacon of Brecon and so of considerably lower rank than his illustrious companion. The two travelled around Wales in 1188 in an effort to win support for the Third Crusade, and Archbishop Baldwin must have made a considerable impact on the locals for them to have named a bridge for him. Gerald was a man of breeding, an intellectual with a flair for writing and a penchant for a colourful legend. He spent his life trying to persuade the Establishment to appoint him Bishop of St David's. Though only one-quarter Welsh, Gerald had a great feel for the country and wished to be Bishop of St David's so that he could then persuade the Pope to confirm him as Archbishop of Wales, a position, he hoped, that would free the Welsh church from the supremacy of Canterbury. His persuasions were in vain and he never achieved his dream, dying a forgotten man in the early 13th century. Gerald might never have been much remembered but for his description of his journey with Archbishop Baldwin. Strangely Gerald does not mention Pont-yr-Esgob or even Partrishow despite its legendary hermit, but he does mention the murder at Dial Carreg (see Note ④ below) and was probably sufficiently nervous about the area just to be glad to be away from it.

③ Partrishow Church

Ffynnon Ishow is the Holy Well of St Ishow, a Celtic hermit and mystic who lived in a solitary monastic cell near the spring here on the side of the Grwyne Fawr valley. He showed kindness and hospitality to any traveller and always attempted to persuade them to a Christian way of life. One day a traveller murdered him for his possessions, a pitiful collection. Years later a rich lady who had contracted leprosy on a journey in Europe stopped to drink from the spring and was cured. She gave money for the building of the well-house that still survives and for an early church to Ishow.

Partrishow church is remote, and this very remoteness means that its interior has survived Puritans and restorers, and is a treasure house of medieval art, despite its plain exterior. The font is huge and certainly the oldest item in the church, being inscribed as having been made in the name of Genillin, a pre-Norman Powys prince. On the west wall is a superb mural, a 'doom figure', Father Time painted as a skeleton with dagger, spade and hour glass. Its position, near the church exit, was a reminder to the departing congregation of their mortality. There are three stone altars, two of which have five consecration crosses – one for each of Christ's wounds – a most remarkable survival of the Elizabethan edict that such altars be destroyed and replaced with tables. The third altar is locked in a side chapel and has six rather than five consecration crosses, a strange number.

The finest piece in the church is the rood screen. These screens were common when there was a gallery with musicians to play at services, the rood being a crucifix attached to the front of the screen. Originally the screen would have extended to the floor, another of its functions having been to stop the congregation's dogs from fouling the altar! The screen at Partrishow is almost complete and is now considered a masterpiece of medieval carving. The carving is a continuous dragon and vine theme, with, probably, the dragon representing evil and the vine representing good. The dragon consumes the vine, but good, as represented in the original by the rood itself, always remained on top. It is often said that the artist was Italian or influenced by Italianate art, but this seems to derive from the idea that no medieval Welshman could have carved a vine!

④ Dial Carreg

Dial Carreg is the Stone of Revenge erected, legend has it, to commemorate the murder of Richard de Clare, a murder mentioned by Gerald of Wales (see Note ② above) and one which made him nervous. De Clare was on his way home to Cardigan after being involved in several skirmishes with the Welsh on behalf of local Marcher lords. The local lord was with him as guide and protector, but de Clare was an arrogant man and not only dismissed him but sent a singer and fiddler ahead of his small group to announce his coming. The party was ambushed and put to the sword. It is not clear where the attack took place. Gerald referring to the spot merely as Grwyne Wood, Nor is this stone original as there was almost certainly a previous one, a larger specimen. Neither is it known who erected the earlier one. To compound the mystery some suggest that the name is not dial (revenge), but deial (dial) and that the stone was simply a marker on a drove route to the Gospel Pas. As dial and deial have almost identical pronunciations there is no way of telling now whether the truth is murder of cattle.

WALK 29 | Llanthony Priory

The Afon Honddu flows through a beautiful wide valley, known as the Vale of Ewyas, from close to Gospel Pass – named from a Welsh legend that St Peter and St Paul came this way in answer to a request from the daughter of Caratacus that they preach the gospel to her people – down to the River Monnow and on into the Wye at Monmouth. The eastern ridge of the Vale is the most easterly of the Black Mountains and is taken by the Offa's Dyke National Trail. The western ridge separates the Vale from the valley of the Grwyne Fawr and offers a fine walk with excellent views of the remains of Llanthony Priory, a romantic ruin beautifully set half-way up the Vale.

Walk Category: Difficult (4½ hours) | Length: 16km (10 miles) | Ascent: 750m (2,450ft) | Maps: Landranger Sheet 161; Outdoor Leisure Sheet 13 | Starting and finishing point: the car-park beside the ruins of Llanthony Priory on the road through the Vale of Ewyas which runs from Llanvihangel Crucorney, on the A465 north of Abergavenny, to Hay-on-Wye

From the car-park go towards the Priory and cross a stile signed for Hatterall Hill. Follow the path beyond to a stream and cross a stile on the left. The stream is running down from Cwm Siarpal (see ① Walter Savage Landor). The path continues through fields and a copse to emerge on to the ridge: go uphill, steeply at first, but then more easily, to reach the ridge top. Turn left here: you are now following a section of the Offa's Dyke National Trail (see Note ⑤ of Walk 36).

Walk past the trig point and continue to 270 319 where a cairn and waymarker stone mark a junction of paths. Turn left and follow

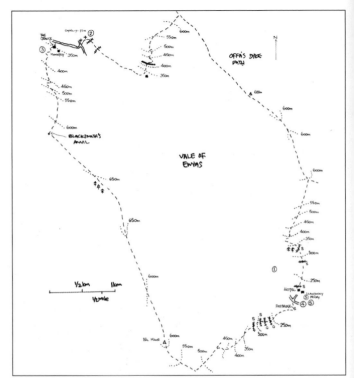

Walk 29: Llanthony Priory

a path which zig-zags down to a wall. Turn right along it, then left over a stile and continue downhill to reach a lane. Turn right and follow the lane to where it turns sharply left. Go ahead here, up steps and over a stile on to a path which crosses fields to reach another lane. Follow this as it heads downhill past a Baptist chapel and St Mary's Church (see ② St Mary's Church) to a road.

Turn right, cross a bridge an--d turn left along a lane signed for the Grange Pony Trekking Centre. Ignore a signed path on the

Llanthony Priory ruins and the eastern Black Mountains ridge

left, beyond which is The Monastery (see ③ Llanthony Monastery) to reach a drive, also left, which leads to several barns. Bear right to pass a house, right, then go left to reach a gate. Go through, up a grass bank and turn right along a path which leads to, and then zig-zags up, the ridge ahead. At the ridge the path reaches a prominent stone known as the Blacksmith's Anvil. Turn left here and follow the ridge over Chwarel y Fan and Bâl-Mawr. To the right (west) on the ridge the view is impeded somewhat by the forestry plantations, but the view left (east) into and over the Vale of Ewyas is excellent.

Beyond Bâl-Mawr the path bears half-left, downhill to a cairn. Now descend left, keeping right at a path fork to reach a cross-roads of paths. Continue downhill on the one – later waymarked – signed for Cwm Bwchel. Two stiles give access to the Cwm Bwchel stream which is heading down, as we are, for the Afon Honddu. Cross a footbridge and go through two gates to reach a footbridge over the Afon Honddu. Follow the lane beyond to the valley road. Turn left, then right to return to the start, passing Llanthony church (see ④ Llanthony church) and Llanthony Priory (see ⑤ Llanthony Priory).

This walk can be extended by continuing along the initial high ridge (and so following the Offa's Dyke National Trail) to reach the trig point on Hay Bluff. Turn left here, following the scarp edge down to Gospel Pass. Now climb along the opposite scarp edge, going over Twmpa (a peak which has a curious alternative name of Lord Hereford's Knob) and continuing along the scarp edge to reach a trig point at 211 334. Here turn left (south-east) along a descending ridge that is shallow at first, but becomes increasingly pronounced. To the left, the cliffs of Tarren yr Esgob fall into the Llanthony valley, while to the right is the reservoir of Grwyne Fawr. The walk rejoins the shorter walk at the Blacksmith's Anvil. This extension adds a further 16km (10 miles) and 320m (1,000ft) of ascent to the walk, but offers the finest excursion on the eastern side of the Black Mountains.

① Walter Savage Landor

Walter Savage Landor, eccentric and poet, was born in 1775 and was first noted for his eccentricity in 1794 when, as a student at Oxford, he allegedly shot at someone with whose reactionary views he had disagreed. His poetry debut waited four more years, for the publication in 1798 of Gebir. Later works were admired for their style and uncompromising ideals, though the romantic nature of much of the work is at odds with the fact that Landor eventually fell out with just about everyone he met and acquired a reputation as a bad-tempered man. He bought the Llanthony estate, including the Priory ruin and a good part of the Vale of Ewyas, in the early 19th century, at first living in that part of the Priory which is now an hotel, but was then the previous owners' shooting lodge. Landor tried a social and agricultural experiment in the Vale, planting – so it is said – 10,000 trees and importing Spanish sheep. Sadly his anti-social habits and lack of agricultural knowledge doomed the project and he left the area, in part to avoid the enemies that his schemes had created for him. He left behind a poem about the place that begins 'Llanthony! An ungenial clime' and ends 'For never is the heart so true; As bidding what we love adieu'. If he was not attempting to be ironic the effect is to exemplify the contradictions of the man. These are nowhere better shown than in his more famous poem:

I strove with none, for none
    was worth my strife;
Nature I loved, and, next to
    Nature, Art;
I warmed both hands before
    the fire of life;
It sinks, and I am ready to
    depart.

It is a lovely piece, but the first line of which would have had many a local smarting with indignation.

② St Mary's Church, Capel-y-ffin

This beautiful little church should not be missed. It has a delightful gallery running along its south and west walls, and stained glass windows which, upon closer examination, are revealed as being of coloured paper rather than coloured glass.

③ Llanthony Monastery

Joseph Leycester Lyne was born in Essex in 1837 and ordained as a deacon of the Anglican Church in 1860.

Shortly after, he came here because he felt that there was a need to re-establish a monastic (Benedictine) way of life in the Anglican Church. For the rest of his life he lectured in both Britain and America to earn money to build his Llanthony Tertia (see Note ⑤ below) as he occasionally called the monastery. Lyne styled himself Father Ignatius and was ordained in his monastery in 1898, when he finally accepted that he would not receive the full support of the Anglican Establishment. He was a saintly, if obsessive man, a man of 'gently simple kind manners' according to Francis Kilvert, the diarist, who met him in the early years of his work at Llanthony.

The monastery was not finished in Lyne's lifetime, and after his death in 1908, it began to fall into disrepair, despite the fleeting fame it achieved when it was claimed that a labourer killed during its construction had been restored of life. Ultimately, in 1924, it was bough by Eric Gill, the engraver and sculptor, and is still owned by his family.

④ *Llanthony Church*

The village name is a shortened form of Llan Dewi Nant Honddu,

St David's Church by the Honddu Stream, because legend has it that St David spent part of his early life here, the first church having been raised on the site of his monastic cell. The Church of St David that occupies the site today is 12th-century and was built so that the altar faces the sun as it rises on the saint's day, 1 March. When the Priory was built the church did not serve as priory church, but became a hospital for both the monks and the local folk. Then, when the Dissolution came, St David's became the parish church again.

⑤ *Llanthony Priory*

One day in the final years of the 11th century a Norman knight, William de Lacy, was riding through the Vale of Ewyas on a hunting trip. Legend has it that de Lacy was weary of war and strife, but whether that was true or not, when he found the remains of St David's cell at Llanthony he recognised the spot as holy and determined to stay for the rest of his life, and to raise an abbey. A monk of the Priory was later to write that William 'laid aside his belt...[and] fine linen...the suit of armour, which

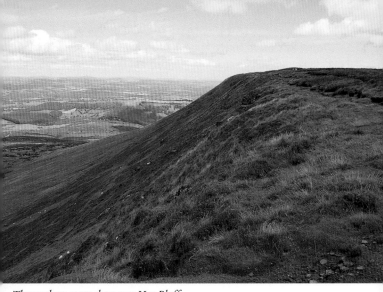

The northern scarp slope near Hay Bluff

before defended him from the darts of his enemies, he still wore as a garment to harden him against the soft temptations of his old enemy, Satan … and continued this hard armour on his body until it was worn out with rust and age.'

Gerald of Wales writes lovingly of the Priory, his account being so much 'first-hand' that many have suggested that he may have spent time there. He recalls a legend of its construction, that the surrounding land was covered with blocks of marble, 'commonly called free-stones, because they are easily split and can be polished with iron tools. The church is built of them and very attractive they make it. They have this remarkable property, that you can search until you are quite exhausted and collect all these free-stones, until none is left and no more could possibly by found, and then, three or four days later, you can look again and there they all are, just as numerous as before, easy to find if you look and there for you to take'. Gerald also recalls that after Roger, Bishop of Salisbury and right-hand man of Henry I, had visited the site he reported that the king's entire treasure could not built a nave as grand as that offered by the surrounding hills.

Despite the tranquil beauty, however, all was not well. In 1136 a local dispute between Welsh clans resulted in the Priory being besieged for a time and the monks were granted permission to leave Llanthony Priory and construct a daughter house – Llanthony Secunda – on the banks of the Severn near Gloucester. The names here, the first and second Llanthony houses, explain why Father Ignatius called his monastery Llanthony Tertia, the third house (see Note ③ above). Very soon the new house had replaced the old. Gerald, who saw the early stages of this replacement, was appalled. Llanthony – the original Priory that is – 'was formerly a happy, a delightful spot, most suited to the life of contemplation, a place from its first founding fruitful and to itself sufficient. Once it was free, but it has since been reduced to servitude, through the boundless extravagance of the English, its own reputation for rich living, uncontrolled ambition, the ever-growing vice of ingratitude, the negligence of its prelates and its patrons and, far worse than all of these, the fact that the daughter house, become a step-mother has odiously and enviously supplanted its own mother'. It is difficult to imagine a more eloquently appalled paragraph than that. Gerald went on to describe the deaths of some of the negligent prelates – Prior William was expelled as unworthy, Prior Clement died of a paralytic stroke and Prior Roger (who stole things from the abbey, Gerald says) died a lingering death.

Of course in Secunda itself they saw it differently. Prima was referred to as the prison. One monk asked who would choose to go and sing to the wolves. Gerald would doubtless be pleased to know that many now come to Prima to marvel at the ruins at the Vale, while of Secunda almost nothing at all remains.

Following the founding of the Severnside house, the Priory here was almost entirely de-populated, the number of monks falling to just five at one stage. The Priory also fell on very hard times and was almost impoverished when it was dissolved by Henry VIII. Today it is a magnificently sited, imposing ruin.

Abergavenny

Though not actually within the boundaries of the Brecon Beacons National Park. Abergavenny is often referred to as the Gateway to the Park. In a sense this is true, as its position in the Usk valley, close to the start of the Heads of the Valleys roads, means that most travellers to the Park from the south or west go close to the town.

Abergavenny is a fine old town, its name causing consternation among many who claim to know a little of the Welsh language. Aber, they say with confidence, means a river mouth, as in Aberystwyth and Aberdyfi. Unfortunately for that theory Abergavenny is a long way from the sea. In fact, *aber* means confluence and while that normally means of a river with the sea, here it means of two rivers. The town is actually named for the smaller of the rivers, the Gavenny stream joining the Usk close to the town.

The Normans fortified the town because of its strategic importance: here the Usk flowed out of its mountain cradle into a broad plain. The castle was held, at an early stage, by William de Braose, a man with a flair for treachery and cruelty, whose murder of a local Welsh chief and his men in the castle after he had invited them to be his guests caused an outrage. Within a year the Welsh had avenged the deaths of their kinsmen by capturing and razing the castle. After this de Braose quarrelled with King John and fled to France. The king imprisoned de Braose's wife and son in Windsor Castle, sending word that they would die of starvation unless he returned. But de Braose did not come back, and mother and child both died. It is a sad story, out of which neither the king nor de Braose emerges with much honour.

A walk around the town will reward the visitor, there being a fine old section with many interesting buildings. Be sure to visit the church where there are tombs to members of the de Braose family and a superb Jesse tree carved from a single 3m (10ft) piece of oak. Such trees were not uncommon, the reclining figure of Jesse, father of David, holding an Old Testament family tree. The Abergavenny figure is special because of its size and exquisite carving, and for being produced from a single trunk. Nothing now remains of the tree itself, though the roots can still be seen in Jesse's left hand.

WALK 30 | Skirrid Mountain

Abergavenny is dominated by two peaks. To the west is Sugar Loaf, an elegant, conical peak named for its shape. It ought to be the Best Walk in this small area around the town, but it is scarred by paths and occasionally overrun by motor bikes to such an extent that no sensitive walker could feel happy on its flanks. Skirrid – the name is an Anglicised version of the Welsh name, Ysgyryd Fawr, a name probably deriving from its deep cleft – is a lower peak, a full 100m (330ft) lower, and less elegantly shaped. It is, however, a less-trekked hill, has a more interesting tale to tell, and commands a fine view because of its position as the last outline of the eastern Black Mountains.

Walk Category: Easy (2 hours) | Length: 6km (3¾ miles) | Ascent: 300m (975ft) | Maps: Landranger Sheet 161; Outdoor Leisure Sheet 13 | Starting and finishing point: The car-park at 329 164 at the base of the hill. This is reached by taking the B4521 road eastward out of Abergavenny, towards Skenfrith. The car-park is on the left (north) side of the road

At the western (Abergavenny) end of the car-park go past the barrier and follow the track to a gate/stile. Beyond, follow the yellow waymarkers to the right, climbing steps and going ahead

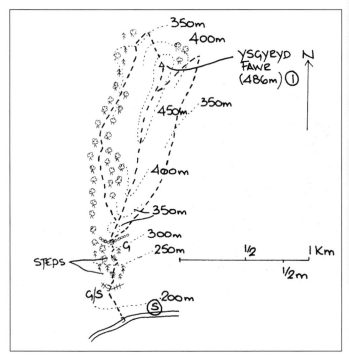

Walk 30: Skirrid Mountain

at an offset crossroads. Cross a track and climb steps to cross another track, continuing to reach a gate. Go through and turn left, following the old wall until it drops away left: continue on the path, crossing another old wall to reach open ground, across which the path rises and falls. Go past a pond, left, bearing right with the hill to cross a stream. Now fork right on an uphill path, heading for the hill crest and what remains of St Michael's Church (see ① Ysgyryd Fawr).

Follow the ridge south, eventually descending the southern spur to reach a wall. Turn right and follow this back to the gate passed on the outward journey. Now reverse the route back to the start.

Skirrid from the west

① **Ysgyryd Fawr**

Skirrid has long been termed the
Holy Mountain, and the summit
area still shows some remains of a
medieval church to St Michael, built
when the hill was a minor pilgrimage
centre. The holiness derived from the
curious cleft in the hill's otherwise
smooth ridge. The cleft is actually
the result of a huge landslip, but legends grew up around its formation.
One story had the hill being rent
apart at the time of the Crucifixion,
while another placed the cleft earlier,

when Noah's Ark landed on the hill
as the waters of the flood receded.
The soil of the hill was also believed
to be holy, one tale claiming that it
had been brought from the Holy
Land itself, while another had
St. Patrick bringing it from Ireland.
Local farmers collected the soil to
sprinkle on their own land, to protect
against crop failure.

The church' was used before the
Reformation, the Mass said there on
Michaelmas being especially impor-
tant. After the Reformation, when
Catholics were persecuted, secret

masses were said in the church, but this is a weatherswept site and the inability of the local Catholics to carry out repairs meant that the church rapidly became ruinous and fell down.

North from the hill is Llanvihangel Crucorney, perhaps the most romantically named village in the area. From the hill the Elizabethan Llanvihangel Court, which lies to the east of the main A465 through the village, can be picked out. The village contains what is claimed to be Wales' oldest inn, The Skirrid, whose inn sign is the Holy Mountain itself, being struck by cleft-producing lightning. The inn is architecturally very interesting, and worth a visit to quench a walk-induced thirst. If you are tempted to stay, be warned, the inn is haunted. Following the Monmouth rebellion Judge Jefferies led a Bloody Assize here, those who were sentenced to death being held in a small room half-way up the stairs before being hanged from a beam above the stairwell. The slab at the bottom of the stairs is reputedly where the hanged bodies were laid out ready for removal and burial. The ghost of the inn is said to be of one of the hanged men.

WALK 31 | # The Monmouthshire and Brecon Canal

Between the base of the scarp slope on the southern side of the Usk valley and the river itself lies the Monmouthshire and Brecon Canal, a navigation from the Golden Age of canals. With the coming of the railways the canal, like most others, fell into disrepair, but it has been lovingly restored to provide a fine recreational waterway that is also a linear nature reserve. Close to Abergavenny is one of the finest sections in the canal's length, and it is that section our walk visits.

Walk Category: Easy (1¾ hours) | Length: 7km (4½ miles) | Ascent: 60m (200ft) | Maps: Landranger Sheet 161; Outdoor Leisure Sheet 13 | Starting and finishing point: At the car-park 262 134 in Govilon, beside the old railway line. Govilon is reached along the B4246 that links Llanfoist, just the other side of the Usk from Abergavenny, to a roundabout on the A465 Heads of the Valleys road. Go left on reaching Govilon on a minor road that crosses the canal. Take the right fork at the Y-junction just over the canal and the car-park is 400m along on the left-hand side

---

At the back of the car-park there is direct access to the old railway (see ① Abergavenny to Merthyr Railway). Go left (east) along the old, now tree-shrouded track, passing under a bridge to a street of houses. Go straight across, and around a barrier to continue behind houses before crossing the road once more. The old track takes a bridge over the canal, then runs beside it for a while before bearing away left. To your left now is the village of Govilon (see ② Govilon). Continue along the old track, ignoring

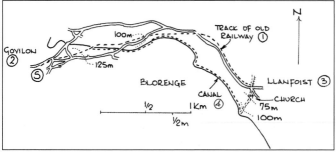

Walk 31: The Monmouthshire and Brecon Canal

a sign, right, for the canal, to eventually reach, a gate into a car park. Ahead is the village of Llanfoist (see ③ Llanfoist).

Turn right across the main road (the B4246) and go up the lane opposite, passing the village church and then going steeply uphill with a stream on the left road edge. Ignore the lane which bears away to the left, continuing to reach steps which lead to the canal (see ④ The Monmouthshire and Brecon Canal). Turn right (west) along the towpath and follow it to a bridge which is used to change banks. In this section the canal is beautifully sited, with the wooded slopes of Blorenge Mountain to one side, and more open country offering views across the Usk valley to the other.

Beyond the bridge the canal passes through a more built-up area as it nears Govilon. Where the old railway – the outward journey – crosses it, leave the towpath to rejoin the track, which is followed back to the start.

① *Abergavenny to Merthyr Railway*

Following the successful expansion of Govilon (see Note ② below) two local companies – called, as was

common at the time, civic pride in technology and industrialisation being high the Merthyr, Tredegar and Abergavenny company and the Newport, Abergavenny and Hereford

Canal bridge, Govilon

Company — combined to build a railway to bring coal from the pits at the valley heads above the scarp slope to the canal. The line followed, in part, the route of an earlier tramway, but also involved some civil engineering work that still brings wide-eyed approval from many a visiting engineer. Near Govilon itself the line climbed an incline of 1 in 34, and a five-mile stretch in the Clydach Gorge, closer to Ebbw Vale and Tredegar, had an average gradient of 1 in 38. Work on the line started in 1858, but had made no great distance before the local companies were bought out by one of the new giants of steam, the London and North-Western Railway Company in 1866. This company pushed the line on to Merthyr Tydfil. The line survived nationalisation, but was reduced to freight only in 1954 and did not survive Dr Beeching's axe in 1958.

For fifteen years the line was left to rot before this small section was bought by Monmouthshire County Council for the National Park Committee to manage. It now forms part of the Govilon to Abergavenny Community Route. Despite limited funds, the route has been made very attractive. The willow trees that arch over the track are not only superbly elegant, but very attractive to insects, so that the bird life on the line is excellent. Blue, Coal, Great, Long-tailed and Marsh tits can all be seen by the lucky visitor, as can several members of the warbler family — most notably the beautiful Blackcap. The limestone that was used as infill for the line has also produced an excellent collection of lime-loving flowers, and wild strawberries grow in abundance.

② Govilon

The name Govilon derives from gefail, forge, so there must have been ironworks here from the earliest days of local industry. The industrialisation of the Clydach gorge, where there were supplies of iron ore and wood for charcoal, meant prosperity for Govilon not as a centre for forging, but because of its position at the base of the scarp. The digging of the scarp base canal (see Note ④ below) meant that the village was the ideal end point for tramways from the gorge. The most impressive of these was that from the Nantyglo iron-works which was completed in 1821. As we have seen above in Note ①, when steam engines replaced the

Thomas James, from the cover of his famous book

horse-drawn trams, Govilon maintained its importance, in part because the local tramway builders had been far-sighted in their choice of gauges. The Bailey tramway – to Nantyglo – was 4'4", while the continuation to Llanvihangel and Hereford was 3'6". When the railway came the wide embankments on which the tramways were laid were sufficient in most places to carry the new lines.

Following the decline of the Clydach iron industry, the decline of canal traffic and the axing of the railway, Govilon became a quieter, more peaceful place. Thos wishing to gain some insight into the way of life of the people when Govilon, and nearby Llanfoist, were busy industrial

The canal at Llanfoist

centres should read Alexander Cordell's Rape of a Fair Country *which is set in the villages in the early years of the 19th century.*

③ Llanfoist

Llanfoist is another village which grew up and found prosperity as a result of its position. There were limekilns beside the church a century or more ago, the rock being brought down from the Pwll-du Quarry on the west side of Blorenge Mountain by a tramway – the Hills Tramway – that ran through a tunnel for most of the way and crossed the old Tods bridge near where our walk joins the canal.

The village was the birthplace of Captain Thomas James, though he is usually known as Captain James of Bristol or of Blaenafon. James was born in the last years of the 16th

century and was an impressionable twenty-year-old when Henry Hudson died after being cast adrift when an expedition to find the North-West Passage failed after the discovery of Hudson Bay. Though he was actually a barrister, James' fascination was such that he became involved in a later attempt at the Passage. Despite his limited experience of the sea James captained the Henrietta Maria on a quest for Passage in 1631. James' venture was financed by Bristolian merchants, and he was in competition with London merchants who financed Luke Foxe in the Charles. The two ships were named for King Charles I and his wife, and the King part-sponsored them and the expedition. The King gave each captain an identical letter which the winner of the race was to deliver to the Emperor of Japan. The letters were in English as it was believed that the Emperor, being a cultured man, would obviously speak the language.

Captain James found and named James Bay, but was then forced to winter on an island in the Bay. The winter was terrible, the crew suffering appallingly from disease and cold. At one point James, in an effort to attract the attention of native Americans on the mainland set fire to a tree. The fire spread and almost roasted his crew, merely adding to their problems. The ship finally reached Bristol again after 18 long months. James wrote a very fine book about the voyage and it is widely believed that it inspired Samuel Taylor Coleridge, though the poet's Rime of the Ancient Mariner was set in more southerly latitudes. Captain James died in 1635.

④ The Monmouthshire and Brecon Canal

When it was originally built the canal here was called the Brecon and Abergavenny and had been constructed to transport agricultural lime and farm produce as much as to provide a carrier for the developing iron industry in the Clydach Gorge.

The building of the waterways during the Golden Age of canals required the setting up of canal companies to survey the route and finance the scheme, and an enabling Act of Parliament to be passed. The Act enabling construction of this canal was passed in 1793, though construction did not start until 1797. In part this was due to the early construction of tramways. The enabling Acts allowed the canal companies to build tramway up to 8 miles from the canal – the 'mileage' – which were very lucrative as usually the company ordered the rolling stock and charged for its use. Local industries could buy and maintain their own rolling stock, but they still had to pay for use of the rival tramways. The canal took fifteen years to build which, since it is only 52km (33 miles) long, seems a very long time. In part this was due to its phased construction, firstly from Pontnewydd to the Monmouthshire Canal at Pontymoel near Pontypool, then the Brecon to Abergavenny section, and finally the last link. In part it was also due to the method of construction – manual digging by navigators, as the labouring men were called. The navigators had only pickaxes, shovels and wheelbarrows, and so hard was the work that the shortened version of their name – 'navvies' – is still a term occasionally applied to anyone involved in hard, physical labour. The bridges and other engineering works on the canal were the responsibility of Thomas Dadford, who also surveyed the route. So good a canal engineer was he that there are only six locks along the canal's length, five of which are in a short section near Llangynidr.

As with all Britain's canals, rail and then road transport made the waterway uncompetitive, and it fell into disrepair. Fortunately the Torfaen Canal Society, together with other interested groups including the National Park and the Nature Conservancy, restored much of the canal and it is now a favourite with pleasure-craft owners and wild life. Along the towpath the walker may see Treecreepers and Nuthatches among the trees, Redpolls feeding among the alders, and, for the very lucky, a glimpse of a Kingfisher. The water itself contains wild life more usually associated with a pond – the canal is, after all, a linear pond. The water plants too are pond plants, with pondweeds and lilies, and reeds and rushes at the margin. Water Forget-me-not can also be found, while away from the water there are other fine plants including Hemlock-water-dropwort, Wall-rue, Spleenwort and Maidenhair ferns.

The Valleys

The Millstone Grit that overlies the carboniferous limestone to the south of the Llangattock escarpment, the rim of the Usk valley, is itself overlaid to the south by rocks of the Coal Measures. The Measures are as much as 2,000m (6,500ft) thick in places and consist of a mixture of shale, sandstone and coal seams. The Measures are sub-divided into Upper, Middle and Lower, the Upper giving the area its dune-shaped plateau, while the Middle and Lower are mined for coal. The coal type and quality varies with position. To the east the coal lies at depth, but is high-quality anthracite and steam coal, while to the west it lies closer to the surface – so close that it can be drift mined, that is from horizontal rather than vertical shafts – and is a coking coal. This distribution explains also the distribution of the steel industry which tended to arise in the west, close to the available coking coal which was used for charging blast furnaces.

A number of parallel river valleys cut into the thick Coal Measures, each flowing from the north-west to the south-east, heading to the coastal plain, to Cardiff and Newport. These valleys, the Ebbw, the Sirhowy, Rhymney, Taff, Cynon and Rhondda, form the most famous industrial area in Britain, a land of myth and legend. The rivers themselves have a pattern that takes little account of the underlying geology and, indeed, even seems on occasions to run counter to the lie of the land and the geological fault pattern. It has been surmised that the Measures were once overlaid by a thick layer of chalk and that the rivers took their courses from the geography of this layer, cutting down into the rocks of the Measures as the chalk was eroded. The rivers exposed coal, as did weathering of the surface in the areas around Blaenafon and Ebbw Vale, and this was almost certainly used as a domestic fuel from earliest days. Not until the Industrial Revolution was the coal exploited on a large-scale commercial basis. The production of coking coal helped the iron and steel industries that had developed around the local iron ore deposits, coke replacing charcoal as a fuel, a happy find as supplies of charcoal were becoming scarce as the local forests were cleared. Steam coal from the western fields drove the trains that came, at a later stage, to shift both coal and the finished steel, and the ports of Cardiff and Newport expanded rapidly. At the time South Wales was at the forefront of technology: Trevethick laid out the world's first railway between Abercynon and Merthyr Tydfil; in Blaenafon high-quality steel was made for the first time from low-phosphorus iron ore; and near Llantrisant in 1853 Dr William Price cremated his dead son, the first such cremation of modern times.

The valleys are steep-sided, the old villages, built at a time when the population level was higher and the area more prosperous, extending ribbon-like along the sides. In them the heroes are not ancient Celts from Arthurian legend or tales of the *Mabinogion,* but more modern men: the Valleys, the capital V here is deliberate, are a land not of Brochfael the Fanged but of Dai the Fly-Half. The people of the Valleys were a tightly-knit folk, suspicious of outsiders. The dangers of mining produced an enviable community spirit, the conditions of work providing a distrust of apparently well-intentioned non-Valley dwellers.

Today the Valleys are a playground for the industrial geologist and the social historian, but are less wonderful for the walker, the ribbon development limiting access to the valleys, the mine spoil making life occasionally difficult on the ridges. Here is a place for visiting, not tramping around. Yet to avoid the area altogether is to ignore some of the most significant places both in Wales and in Welsh history. For that reason a slight departure in format is required. Our Best Walk will visit not the country, but a town.

WALK 32 | Blaenafon

Around the 1780 Blaenafon – the Top of the River, the river in this case being the Afon Llwyd – was an area with a few scattered farms, none of them very big, and none of the farmers very prosperous. One hundred years later there were almost 10,000 people living in one of Britain's foremost industrial towns. At around the same time two men working in Blaenafon's ironworks solved a long-outstanding problem in steel making, giving the town new impetus. By the early years of the 20th century Blaenafon had grown into a prosperous town of 13,000 people. The 1920s brought decline, as they did to almost every town in Britain, but in Blaenafon the decline was nearly terminal. Today the town has fewer then half its peak population and there are still areas of decay and dereliction. Yet within a small area there are some of the finest industrial archaeological sites in Britain, sites which alone would make Blaenafon worth a visit. But there is more here, even if it is less tangible, for Blaenafon is also the essence of South Wales. Here there was a pit and a steel works, they prospered, they declined, they closed. It was a joke that the industries of South Wales closed on Friday nights and reopened as museums on Monday mornings, a joke often thought by the locals to be in very bad taste. But we should be grateful for the existence of the museum sites and buildings of Blaenafon, to show how the Valleys used to be.

The walk described here is a short one, through a small section of the town and does not really fit well into the style used for describing the others. Interesting points will therefore be described in the text.

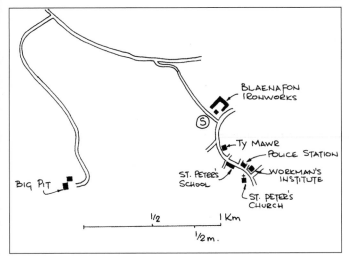

Walk 32: Blaenafon

Walk Category: Easy (1 hour) | Length: 4km (2½ miles) | Ascent: 40m (130ft) | Maps: Landranger Sheet 161; Outdoor Leisure Sheet 13 (though only the map given with the walk is necessary) | Starting and finishing point: The car park across from the Ironworks

The first thing that catches the eye in the car-park (and how could it fail to do so?) is the huge, but modern, steel press. The second is the name of the nearby industrial estate, Gilchrist Thomas. By the mid-19th century the work of Bessemer and Siemens meant that steel had replaced iron as the major constructional metal. Unfortunately, steel could only be produced from low-phosphorus ore, a high phosphorus content making the steel too brittle, and this comprised only about 10 per cent of known ores. The problem of how to use high-phosphorus ore exercised the minds of steel-making chemists for about a quarter of a century. Sidney Gilchrist

Thomas, though the son of a Welshman, was a clerk at London's Metropolitan Police Courts and a keen, but amateur, chemist. For years he worked on the problem of high-phosphorus steels with a small furnace in his rooms, eventually persuading his cousin, Percy Gilchrist, the chemist at Blaenafon's ironworks, to help him. The two carried out a series of experiments at the site – Sidney Gilchrist Thomas travelling down at weekends to work – and in 1878 solved the problem by use of a chemically basic slag rather than the acidic one in use at the time. After the discovery Thomas – who also had the good sense to realise that the process's high phosphorus residue was useful agriculturally – was feted throughout the world, meeting, and selling his patents, to Andrew Carnegie. Sadly Thomas failed to receive the full benefit of his fortune, dying at just thirty-five in 1885. The naming of the estate is a fine memorial to the man, though elsewhere in the world his name is held in higher esteem that it is in his own country.

The Ironworks, reached across the road from the car-park and now in the hands of Cadw, was the first to have been built at Blaenafon and dates from 1789. There are five blast furnaces built into the side of the hill so that they could be charged from above, and the superb remains of a balance tower. This was used to transfer pig iron to the tramways on Blorenge Mountain, water being diverted into boxes that, when full, were heavy enough to raise trolleys of iron up the towers. At the tower base the boxes were emptied, the heavier trolleys then hauling them back up. Also on the site are rows of workers' cottages, tiny two-up, two-down terraced cottages. In one of these one ironworker's wife raised nineteen children, and it must be remembered that these cottages were for the more important workers. The life of all the workers, but especially of the lowest paid, was harsh and as the company controlled the only shop there was both poverty and resentment.

St Peter's Church, Blenafon

One target for resentment is seen when we leave the Ironworks – but first look out for the Drum and Monkey opposite the works, a pub made famous by Alexander Cordell in *Rape of a Fair Country*. Go right from the Ironworks, following the road as it falls and curves left. On the left side is Ty Mawr, the Big House, built for one of the Ironworks' owners and a sharp contrast with the tiny cottages at the site. Blorenge Mountain was, at the time, Britain's most southerly grouse moor and in season Ty Mawr would be full of shooting guests. The men in the works, forbidden to join a union even though an employers' association existed to help maximise profits, must have been resentful indeed.

Further on, but to the right, is St Peter's School built by Sarah Hopkins, sister of Samuel, an early ironworks' owner. She built the first school in 1816 to his memory, adding an inscription, in Latin, that noted her brother's 'benevolent intentions…towards his Glenavonians'. The gesture was a fine one, and the school had 120 pupils when it first opened, but not everyone shared Sarah's opinion of her brother's benevolent intentions. The word Glenavonians is interesting, implying that a non-local carver was used, one who had no idea of the town's name and misread his instructions. Later buildings on the site were added in the mid-19th century.

Beyond the school there is a fine building to the left, a police station and courthouse, built in 1867. Opposite is St Peter's Church, a remarkable building of 1805. The church is a simple structure of local stone but the window frames and sills, the tomb covers and the font are of cast iron. The cast iron font is a unique feature. Inside there are memorials to the Hopkins and Hill families, the Ironworks' owners, while the churchyard holds the graves of many Midlanders brought here in the early days when there was a shortage of local labour.

The next building to the left is perhaps the finest memorial to the workers of Blaenafon, the Workmen's Hall and Institute. The building, a sturdy, confident structure with just a hint of sensitive decoration, was completed in 1894, paid for by contributions from steelworkers and miners. The building held an auditorium for concerts and shows, a games room and, most remarkable of all, a library and reading room.

The Hall is a good place to stop, though there are other fine buildings, most notably the Moriah Chapel from 1888 and the earlier Horeb Chapel of 1862, but one more site should be visited. Most people will go by car as Big Pit, the National Mining Museum is over 2km (1¼ miles) from the Ironworks. The walk to the site is straightforward enough, but can be depressing.

Big Pit itself, the shaft that visitors can descend, was sunk in 1860, but forms part of a complex of coal mines that were first sunk to supply the coal needs of the Blaenafon Ironworks. When the mine finally closed in 1980 it was the oldest working mine in the South Wales coalfield. Today it is often alive with the sound of children's laughter. In 1840 a Parliamentary Commission found many of the most crucial functions in the mine being carried out by children who had little to laugh about. One boy, a veteran of three years in the pit at the age of seven, smoked a pipe all day in order to stay awake. The Commission also found that in 1838 fifty-eight children aged under thirteen had been killed in mine accidents. The Commission tried to have children banned from the mines, an action strongly opposed by the government who claimed that such a move would bring about a collapse of the industry. Ironically, when the law was passed and an inspector turned up at Blaenafon to ensure compliance, he was besieged by a crowd of local folk angry at the loss of income to their families.

The Wye Valley and the Forest of Dean

The Wye is the most beautiful river valley in Britain. From Plynlimon, where the river starts as it means to go on, in a well-defined valley, to a point south of Chepstow where it joins the Severn and the sea, the Wye has not one industrial blemish. So unpolluted is the river and so untarnished the countryside it flows through that its whole length has been designated a Site of Special Scientific Interest. In its lower reaches, south from Ross-on-Wye, the river flows in a sometimes high-sided, but always deeply wooded valley where over 690 native species of tree and shrub grow. In this area the river is flowing through limestone country, and here it also forms the border between England and Wales. In its upper reaches the river is wholly Welsh, flowing out of the mountains of Plynlimon and into a wooded section south of Builth Wells that is one of its finest sections. From Hay-on-Wye the river's middle section is wholly English, meandering across the Herefordshire plain.

As a tourist attraction the Wye was 'discovered' by the Revd William Gilpin, high priest of the Picturesque – see the introduction to Walk 36 below – with his book *Observations on the Rive Wye and Several Points in South Wales* published in 1782. Gilpin made a trip down the river and soon the Wye tour became <u>the</u> thing to do if you had pretensions to being someone in late 18th- and early 19th-century society. The Wye Tourers were transported by boat, starting from Ross-on-Wye, as the river was deemed unnavigable by boats loaded with gentlefolk north of the town. In a rowing boat equipped with six or eight sturdy locals the Tourers would watch the river go by, sketching perhaps if the mood took them, from beneath the cover of their protective awning. At suitable times an on-boat or on-shore picnic would be taken, hampers laden with food and wine being brought for the purpose. At the end of Day One, the Tourers would spend the night in Monmouth. On Day Two they would finish their Tour at Chepstow.

Today's Wye tourer must paddle his own canoe, and since the Wye is, from Glasbury to Chepstow, a public river the canoeist can proceed at his leisure. The canoe trip is one of the best ways of seeing the river. It is a gentle, easy enough journey, the only rapids being at Monnington and Symonds Yat, and these offering more fun than problems. And if you are alone in early summer, on the river as the sun is rising, with the birds and the damsel flies, it is a fine place to be.

Those keener on seeing the valley than the river at constant close quarters will find it well supplied with walks.

It seems strange to include an area of England in a book on Wales, but the Forest of Dean has always been a mysterious place, neither England nor Wales, just Dean. Also, since the logical return route of Walk 36 is on the English side of the Wye and in the Forest, it seemed a shame not to include just one Walk that explored this most ancient landscape. Today the Forest covers about 11,000 hectares (27,000 acres), just a fraction of its total area when early man first cleared the trees for his farming. It was later development that reduced the forest's site, the discovery of iron ore in the forest bringing a need for charcoal, the trees being felled in huge numbers to produce it. The Normans checked this destruction by making Dean a Royal Forest, but by the Middle Ages iron-making with charcoal-fired blast furnaces was in full production. Henry VIII realised the importance of the Forest as a supplier of trees for the Royal Navy, but his protection laws fell into disrepute and a 17th century iron master, Sir John de Winter, started to destroy trees at an alarming rate. It has been calculated that had it not been for the Civil War, de Winter would have felled the forest, converting it en masse into charcoal. During the Commonwealth the enormous damage that had been done to the Forest was recognised and trees – mostly oaks – were planted by the thousand. The remaining Forest was fenced to prevent animals from eating seedlings – an action that caused riots among the locals – and slowly recovered. Nelson visited the forest two years before his death at Trafalgar and his criticism of its state did much to persuade the authorities into a new programme of planting and protection. The Free Miners – men who lived in the Forest and claimed the right to mine coal and iron-ore at any site of their choosing, a right they jealously guarded, passing the freemanship down from father to son -were required to pay for any trees they felled for pit props, and the destruction of trees was halted. It is doubtful, though, whether the decline in Forest area would have been so easily halted if coking coal had not replaced charcoal in blast furnaces, or the iron-clad battleship not replaced the man o'war.

Today the Forest is a mix of the ironically necessary fast-growing conifers and ancient woodland, still mainly oaks. There are small herds of fallow deer – at one time there was an attempt to wipe out the deer stock in order to stop poachers who damaged trees and saplings – and a fine collection of woodland birds.

WALK 33 | Boughrood

After it has left Plynlimon the Wye flows in a deep, but less steep-sided, valley through Llangurig to Rhayader. From there the river is followed by the Upper Wye Valley Walk, a fine route that takes the walker 55km (35 miles) to Hay-on-Wye. Below Builth Wells the route hugs the river bank in the finest section of river scenery in the early part of the Wye's journey. The route, like the river, is linear rather than circular, but a return is possible using quiet country lanes where the walker is usually alone with the hedgerows.

Walk Category: Easy (2½ hours) | Length: 10km (6¼ miles) | Ascent: 30m (100ft) | Maps: Landranger Sheet 161; Outdoor Leisure Sheet 13 | Starting and finishing point: The village of Llyswen, on the A470 from Builth Wells to Bronllys/Talgarth

From the village (see ① Llyswen) go north-west, back towards Builth Wells, for about 500m and take road beside the inn signed for Boughrood. The lane to the left passed shortly is where the return route re-enters Llyswen. The Wye is first sighted from the Boughrood Bridge, a real appetiser for the second half of the walk. When Boughrood is reached go left, following the road signed for Painscastle to the church (see ② Boughrood). The churchyard offers a change to escape from road walking for a few metres. Beyond the church the road doglegs left and right, and then left again as we take a lane north-west towards Llanstephan and Aberedw (see ③ Aberedw). The church at Llanstephan is worth a visit, if only for the views from it and the superb yew trees.

Beyond the lane to Llanstephan, and the turning off to Aberedw, our route crosses Llanstephan Bridge. The bridge is a

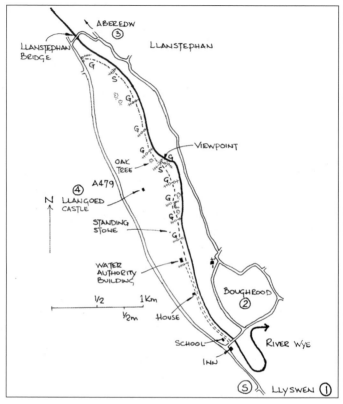

Walk 33: Boughrood

glorious construction of wood and iron and offers a fine view of
the river. Now to reach the river go left along the verge of the
main road for 200m to reach a signed path to the left. Beyond a
gate follow the fence to the river and go right (south-east) along
it. The bank itself can occasionally be followed, but usually the
easiest walking is at the field edge. This is a superb piece of country. The river itself is at its prettiest and ahead is the striking outline of Mynydd Troed, climbed by Walk 25. In spring the fields

The Wye at Boughrood

are carpeted with bluebells and celandine, the broom is purest yellow and woodpeckers drum away in the trees. A magnificent oak tree is passed just before a stile, beyond which a gate in the fence to the left gives access to a river viewpoint with a seat. A rutted lane gives the way for a few metres and a gate leads to an old wooden hut and a superb avenue of sweet chestnut trees. In addition to other oaks and chestnuts there are birch, hazel, hawthorn, holly, sycamore and, of course, willow. To the right the eye is taken by Llangoed Castle (see ④ Llangoed Castle) and a tall, elegant standing stone.

Beyond a small pier the walk reaches a metalled lane past a pumping station, a lane that is followed to Llyswen. In the final few metres past the school the smell of wild garlic can be overpowering at the right (?) time of the year.

① Llyswen

The village is named for a llys-wen, a white court, built here in the 9th century by Roderic, a prince of southern Wales. The court was said to have been the finest in the whole of Wales though nothing of it now remains. At the time of Roderic the Celtic Welsh still practised gavelkind, *the division of a father's land between his sons on his death, a continual source of trouble in Welsh history as the sons often fought for total control. Roderic divided his kingdom as equally as he could, and decreed that each son should have a court where disputes between them could be settled amicably. One of these courts was here at Llyswen. After his death, however, the sons forgot all their fine promises and civil war broke out. One victim of the wars was Llyswen which lost not only its court, but its place of importance in Welsh affairs.*

Late in the 18th century the village was briefly famous again when John Thelwall, the radical who had been tried for sedition, moved into a local farm. There he was visited by William Wordsworth and his sister Dorothy. At that time the poet, who was later to become such a pillar of the Establishment, was himself a radical young man.

② Boughrood

Boughrood has an English-looking name and it comes as a surprise to many visitors to find that it is pronounced boc-rue-id, *the name actually deriving from the Welsh* bach rhyd, *little ford. The ford here, and, later, the bridge, once carried the visitor between the counties of Breconshire and Radnorshire, before both were swallowed by the new Powys. There are two castles in* the village, one a Norman motte, the other a 19th century private house once occupied by Francis Fowkes who had fifteen children by a London actress called Mary Lowe, without taking the time to marry her, after returning from making a fortune in India where, legend has it, he had left another fine brood with an Indian woman whom he also forgot to marry.

Boughrood church is Victorian, an earlier church having all but fallen down through neglect. It was mentioned by Francis Kilvert, the famous diarist, who noted that the choir sat on the altar, there being nowhere else, and were accompanied only by a drum. At about the same time a published guide to the local area suggested avoiding the village where there was no fit lodging for a lady, though it did note that the view of the Wye from the bridge was a fine one, and for it 'a venial trespass should be risked'.

③ *Aberedw*

The village is famous for the part it played in the last days of Llywelyn the Last. A cave among the rocky outcrops above the village is known as Llywelyn's Cave and is reputedly where the last Prince of Wales of Welsh royal lineage spent his final days. From it he rode to Cilmery a little way from Builth Wells, where he was killed by one Adam Francton, an English soldier who had no idea of who it was he had speared. When he was told he returned to cut off Llywelyn's head so that the English king could exhibit it on a spike at the Tower of London, crowned with ivy. Llywelyn's headless body was spirited way, probably to Abbey Cwmhir.

④ *Llangoed Castle*

The building is not correctly called a castle, though there is a local story that it does indeed stand on the site of a medieval fortress. It dates, in fact, from the early years of the twentieth century and is a huge mansion designed by Sir Clough Williams-Ellis who is (rightly) more famous for his Italianate folly village Portmeirion in North Wales. The castle is not open to the public.

WALK 34 | Symonds Yat

When the Wye Tourer left Goodrich Castle with its fine position, its romantic ruins and the ghosts of a young couple who drowned in the Wye beside it as they struggled to escape the twin perils of the Civil War and an irate father, they were treated to two huge, meandering river bends. The first took them 5 river-kilometres (3 miles) to reach Welsh Bicknor about 700 land-metres away. The second was even bigger and it took closer to 7 river-kilometres (about 4½ miles) to circumnavigate the 500 metre land neck of Symonds Yat. The Tourers did not stay in the boats here, preferring to climb Yat Rock for the views. Our route also climbs the Rock, after descending through the Forest to reach the Wye and following it past its famous section of rapids.

Walk Category: Easy/Intermediate (2½ hours) | Length: 8km (6 miles) | Ascent: 200m (650ft) | Maps: Landranger Sheet 162; Outdoor Leisure Sheet 14 | Starting and finishing point: The Pay and Display Car Park at Symonds Yat reached along the B4432 from Christchurch

From the disabled car park, follow the yellow waymarker arrows which lead you southward through the forest. The path is level and surfaced, though there are occasional sections which may be a little muddy after rain. The trail exits on to a road. Turn right and follow the road to the Bracelands camp/caravan site.

Now continue to follow the yellow waymarkers, descending through High Highmeadow Woods (see ① Highmeadow Woods), steeply in places, but always straightforwardly. Follow the trail all the way to the river (see ② The Slaughter). Now turn right and follow a riverside path to Symonds Yat (see ③ Symonds Yat).

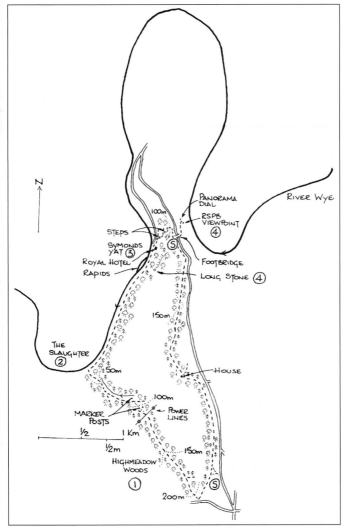

Walk 34: Symonds Yat

As the village is neared the impressive Royal Hotel is reached. On the hotel's far side, follow the initially (and, later, occasionally) stepped track signed with yellow waymarkers which climbs up through more beautiful woodland to reach the log cabin refreshment kiosk close to the car park. Now follow the broad trail ahead to reach a footbridge over the main road and a narrow path which soon reaches Yat Rock (see ④ Yat Rock).

Retrace the path from the Rock to the car-park.

① *Highmeadow Woods*

Highmeadow Woods cover 1,400 hectares (3,500 acres) and are a mixed wood with over twenty species of tree including some superb beeches. The wood is also home to one of the last two large herds of Fallow Deer in the Forest of Dean – the other is in the woods near Speech House – and the lucky visitor may catch sight of them. They are nervous creatures, rarely leaving the full cover of the woods during the day, and are usually seen either at dawn or dusk. It is difficult to know whether you will be lucky or otherwise if they catch sight of the herd of wild boar illegally released into the wood in 2005. The herd is said to have been 'semi-domesticated' though quite what that means in practice is difficult to judge. The wood's bird life is excellent, with five species of tit, Tree-creepers, Nuthatches, all three

species of woodpecker, Redstarts, Pied Flycatchers, Wood Warblers and even Tree Pipits. The patient or very lucky visitor may also catch sight of that most elusive forest bird, the Hawfinch.

The woods are part of the ancient Forest and have remained unchanged for centuries. Not surprisingly, therefore, there are mythical sites. At 541 141 is the Suckstone, a huge monolith (single stone), one of the largest in Britain. Estimates of its weight vary, but it could be as much as 400 tons, which is certainly heavy for a pebble. Close by is Near Harkening Rock, a brother to Far Harkening Rock closer to the river. No satisfactory explanation of the names exists, but they are said to have been used by gamekeepers listening for poachers. In the section of the wood south of the A4136 is the Buckstone, at 542 123 (and easily reached by a short walk from the village of Staunton). It is, or rather was, a logan rock, that is a rock so well-balanced that it can be rocked gently by the slightest pressure. Sadly, vandals in 1885 overturned it and so it no longer rocks, but before then its balance was so perfect that even gentle breezes moved it. The rocking of logans was supposed to foretell the future and many legends have grown up around the stone, for example if you walk three times around it at dawn any wish you make will come true, or that it was a sacrificial stone of the druids.

② The Slaughter

In the 10th century Eric Bloodaxe, leader of a Viking band, landed at Beachley, where the old Aust Ferry also landed after crossing the Severn, and close to where the first motorway Severn Bridge still touches land on the Welsh side. Eric's band raped and pillaged their way to Symonds Yat, camping there on the protected high land which offered them a clear view of an advancing army. And indeed a Saxon army did come, marching up the Wye in pursuit. The Vikings poured down on the Saxons and in the battle that followed so many

were killed that the site of the encounter became known as The Slaughter. Such is one, apparently fairly unlikely, version of how this area of the Wye's left bank came by its name. Another version prefers its battle to be between the Romans and retreating Celtic tribesmen under the leadership of Caratacus. On the other bank, and a little to the west, is Little Doward hill fort where the Silures and Ordovices – men from tribes whose names are now used to describe types of rock in the geology of Wales and the world – are said to have camped before the battle. Certainly Caratacus did form an army of Celtic men, and did fight the Romans in South Wales. He was finally betrayed and captured in AD51 and spent the rest of his life as an honoured guest of Rome, but there is no direct evidence of a battle here on the Wye's banks.

Neither of these stories – nor another, less common one that deals with a Civil War skirmish – seems likely to be responsible for the name. The villages of Upper and Lower Slaughter in the nearby Cotswolds are now believed to derive their name from the Saxon for sloe trees, which would also seem to be a more likely explanation of the name here.

The Wye from Yat Rock

③ Symonds Yat

Most experts agree that the Yat part of the village's name is derived from gate, the Saxon word for a track. About Symonds there is much less agreement. Some would like to see it deriving from seaman, to indicate that the village was on an invasion route of the Vikings, a useful tie-up *with one derivation of the name, The Slaughter (see Note ② above). Others have a more prosaic explanation, seeing the name as deriving from Robert Symonds, a 17th century High Sheriff of Herefordshire.*

The village is a tourist trap, all ice-creams and boat trips, but is undoubtedly pretty. The old ferry across the Wye – the river divides

the village into two parts, the western half being slightly less brash – is interesting, the flat-bottomed boat being man-hauled across by means of an overhead cable.

The rapids in the Wye just south of the village are a favourite spot for canoeists. The natural obstructions in the river (see Note ④ below) have been added to, to form a series of tight channels which offer an exciting, but quite safe, ride.

④ Yat Rock

One Wye Tourer noted that the climb from the river to Yat Rock 'though a work of some toil, will reward the curious observer'. The suggestion was that the Rock was

2,000ft high, a great exaggeration of the actual height of 500ft (150m).

The best explanation for the long gorge that takes the Wye around the rock is that the long meander was formed when the sea level was around 180m (600ft) higher than it is now, and that when the level dropped the river cut down into the rock, leaving behind a raised table of limestone. The upper bands of the limestone include one of Lower Dolomite, a band of rock with vertical jointing whose weathering has produced a series of detached towers. The collapse of one helped produce the Wye rapids, while another has produced Long Stone, the tower of rock, dripping with vegetation, that pokes its way through the trees and is so eye-catching from Symonds Yat village.

On the opposite side of the Rock from Long Stone is the famous view-point that the Wye Tourers toiled to reach. Today's visit is assisted in admiring the view by a panorama dial, but it is the Wye that draws the eye, virtually the whole of the meander being visible from here. Here too is an RSPB observation point, a telescope (in season) helping the visitor to a better view of a nest site of a pair of Peregrine Falcons who have frequented the Rock for several years. These magnificent birds, slate grey and very quick, have been badly persecuted by egg collectors and others seeking young birds for training in falconry, and the Society's protection work at this and other sites is to be applauded. A peregrine stooping in pursuit of a pigeon, its usual prey, is one of nature's truly great sights and it would have been a tragedy if it was lost from British skies.

WALK 35 | The Heart of the Forest

The Forest of Dean is criss-crossed with paths, and traversed by unfenced roads. In the sense that this gives almost complete access to the forest, and because – dare one say it – one tree looks like another, there is no Best Walk: almost, perhaps, no need for a Best Walk. But near Speech House there are several interesting sites which may be linked to produce a memorable afternoon.

Walk Category: Intermediate (3½ hours) | Length: 14km (8¾ miles) | Ascent: 250m (800ft) | Maps: Landranger sheet 162; Outdoor Leisure Sheet 14 | Starting and finishing point: The car-park close to Speech House, at 622 122

From the car park, head west, walking parallel with the road (on your left), and soon reaching an obelisk (see ① Obelisk). Now turn left to cross the road, and to take the road, signed for Park End and Blakeney, which runs down the side of Speech House (see ② Speech House), passing, to the right, an oak planted by HM The Queen during a visit to the Forest. After about 300m bear left along the track into another car park, going through a gate to reach a straight track (the Spruce Ride) through the forest. Now look for a small lake (Speech House Lake) through the trees to the right: it is about 600m from the road, but in summer can be easy to miss. Go half-right here, taking a path along the lake edge. Go right at the lake's southern end, but then, soon, turn left along a narrow path through bushes, walking with a stream on your left to reach a path junction. Turn right, uphill, going through a gate to a road.

Go straight across, following the track opposite. Go through another gate and continue to a junction of five paths. The single

The Heart of the Forest obelisk

oak and the stump here are all that remain of three fine oaks which were known as the Three Brothers. Take the second track to the right (that is, turn right, not first, sharp right) and follow a green waymarked path going downhill. Go through a gate and continue through fine woodland (the bluebells are superb here in spring) to reach the track of a disused railway (see ③ Severn and Wye Railway). Turn right along the old track, with the southern Cannop Pond to your left (see ④ Cannop Ponds).

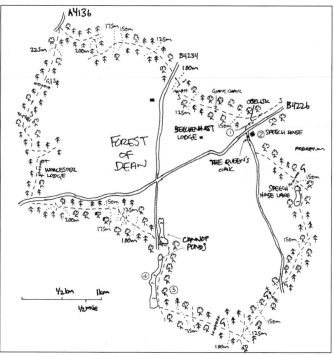

Walk 35: The Heart of the Forest

Continue along the track past the pond end to reach the northern pond. Now turn left, following yellow waymarkers, crossing a footbridge and reaching a road. Cross and go through the car park opposite, continuing on a track which soon turns right. Here go ahead, following a path, waymarked by yellow arrows, which climbs through fine forest, crossing two tracks before reaching a third. Turn right along this one, following it to a barrier. Go past to reach a path junction. Go ahead, then take right-hand path at a fork, continuing to another path junction. Turn right and walk down to a road opposite a sign for the Worcester Lodge camp site. Follow the site lane opposite, but where it bears right, follow the narrow, yellow-waymarked path ahead which goes to the left of the camp site. At the northern site boundary bear right to join a grassy track. Follow this to a track junction. Turn sharp left to follow a meandering track for about 800m. Now where the track bears right, go left – look for the yellow waymarkers – on a path to a stile. Go over and on to a gate with a stile to the left. Follow the track beyond, ignoring a stile on the right, to reach a track junction: go straight ahead to reach a road.

Do not cross the road: instead, turn sharp right along a track signed for Speech House, with views to the right of the Black Mountains. The track goes downhill: at the bottom, turn left (opposite a stile on the right), following a path to a track. Turn left, downhill, following the yellow waymarkers across several track junctions to reach a road.

Cross and continue ahead, using stepping stones to cross the Cannop Brook, then climbing uphill to cross the old railway track again (see, also, Note ③). Go over a stile and follow the uphill track beyond, keeping ahead at a cross-tracks to reach a giant chair (see ⑤ Forest Sculpture). From the chair there is a fine view of the local forest.

Follow the track past the chair – it is to your right – to reach a stile. Do not go over: instead, turn right and walk uphill. Speech House is ahead now: turn left to return to the start.

---

① *Obelisk*

As the inscription notes, the obelisk was erected at the point which was traditionally considered to the centre of the forest. It was erected in 1957 by Viscount Bledisloe to commemorate both his 90th birthday and his 50 years as a verderer (see Note ② below).

② *Speech House*

Prior to the Norman Conquest the Forest of Dean was, to all except those who lived in it, a curious, mysterious place, a wedge of densely forested land between the Severn and the Wye in which lived solitary people making a living from charcoal burning or mining, their lives and interactions with each other and the outside world governed by a complex series of forest laws laid down, it would seem, in part to control exploitation of the forest itself, in part to prevent exploitation of themselves. The Norman kings changed all this by making the forest a Royal Forest, a hunting ground where the king alone had the right to kill. Penalties for poaching and for sheep grazing were high, but the charcoal burners and miners were not banished, just controlled. To exercise this control a system of officials was set up and these heard complaints and disputes at the Court of Verderers, a verderer being one who made a living from the vert, literally the green, the forest itself. The Court was held every forty days, and as it was also known as the Speech Court because of the rights to speech of the Verderers, it was held at what was known as the Speech House. The current house dates from the time of Charles II who used it as a hunting lodge. Speech House is now an hotel. The Court of Verderers is still held here, though no longer at forty day intervals, the courtroom, the timbered dining-room, being open to visitors.

Beside the hotel, and also close to the starting car-park, is an arboretum with a good collection of both trees and shrubs.

③ Severn and Wye Railway

The Forest of Dean has long been a mining area. Coal is the most famous of the minerals mined, but iron ore was also extensively mined from the 16th to the 19th centuries. Building stone was quarried at several locations and limestone was crushed for agricultural lime. As elsewhere all early transportation was by pack-horse, but by the start of the 19th century tramways were being built. An early one was that linking the great waterways of the Severn and the Wye, opened in 1813 between Lydbrook and Lydney. This line had many side tracks to mines and quarries, and was later taken over as a fully fledged railway carrying steam trains. A side line was also built to link it with Cinderford and on towards Gloucester. The old track crossed here is on the Cinderford link.

④ Cannop Ponds

The ponds were created by damming the Cannop Brook in the early 19th century to provide water for a 50ft waterwheel which itself powered the

The forest in autumn

Park end ironworks. The Parkend
site was one of the most important in
the forest, producing around
200,000 tonnes of iron over its
life. By the end of the 19th century
dwindling supplies of local ore and
competition from other sites meant
the end of local smelting. The Ponds
are now a popular local beauty spot.

⑤ *Forest sculpture*

*Several years ago an exhibition of
permanently positioned sculptures in
the Forest was organised by Bristol's
Arnolfini Gallery in conjunction
with the Forestry Commission, wth
additional funding from the Henry
Moor Foundation, the Elephant*

Trust and the Carnegie United
Kingdom Trust. The idea behind the
exhibition was to commission artists
to produce works that interpreted the
forest. Each artist was given a site
and produced a work that will
remain in situ permanently. Indeed
in the case of some of the works the
use of natural materials means that
they will eventually decay and are,
therefore, a part of the 'living' fabric
of the forest itself. Some of the sculptures are startling, some amusing,
but all are thought-provoking. The
giant chair is the work of
Magdalene Jetelova.

WALK 36 | The Lower Wye

In its lowest reaches the Wye Valley is well-served with paths. The Offa's Dyke National Trail joins the river at Monmouth and travels down the left, eastern, bank, while the (Lower) Wye Valley Walk links Hereford to Chepstow. From Ross to Redbrook the Valley Walk hops from bank to bank, but south of Redbrook it takes the right (western) bank. There is, therefore, the chance of a fine walk that is waymarked all along its length. If that walk links Tintern to Chepstow it has the added advantage of visiting one of Britain's most beautifully set abbeys and one of its most commanding castles. Here, too, there is superb woodland and a collection of fine viewpoints.

Walk Category: Difficult (5 hours) | Length: 20km (12½ miles) | Ascent: 500m (1,650ft) | Maps: Landranger Sheet 162; Outdoor Leisure Sheet 14 | Starting and finishing point: Numerous, but the best ones are at the 'terminal' points, at Chepstow or, and better, at the car-park for Tintern Abbey on the A466 Chepstow to Monmouth road

From the Abbey car-park (see ① Tintern Abbey) go right (north) along the main road for 250m to a lane, left. Do not take this, but instead go hard left on a narrower lane – signed with the yellow arrow and yellow dot of the Wye Valley Walk – that runs back almost parallel to the main road. This lane rises steadily to reach woodland, continuing as a path through the woods to a stile and open countryside. Ahead is another piece of woodland through which a path threads its way to Wyndcliff (see ② Wyndcliff). Here, having followed a road for a short section, the walk takes a

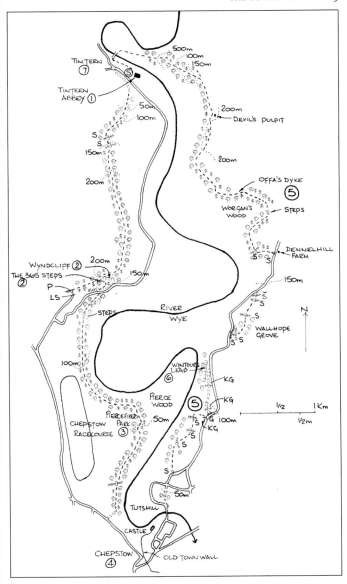

TINTERN ⑦
TINTERN ABBEY ①
500m
100m
150m
50m
100m
S
S
150m
200m
DEVIL'S PULPIT
200m
200m
OFFA'S DYKE ⑤
WORGAN'S WOOD
STEPS
DENNELHILL FARM
S S
WYNDCLIFF ②
THE 365 STEPS ②
P
LS
200m
150m
STEPS
RIVER WYE
150m
S
S
S S
WALLHOPE GROVE
S S
N
100m
WINTOURS LEAP ⑥
KG
PIERCE WOOD
KG
PIERCEFIELD PARK
⑤
G 100m
50m
S S
KG
CHEPSTOW RACECOURSE ③
S
S
½   1 Km
½m
S
S
50m
TUTSHILL
50m
CASTLE
CHEPSTOW ④
OLD TOWN WALL

track that reaches the car-park at the base of Wyndcliff, and continues out of the car-park on a track to the main A466. As an alternative to this route the 365 Steps can be used to descend to the base of Wyndcliff, from where an obvious path from the bottom of the steps is followed through stunning woodland to the car-park. The Steps are not for the faint-hearted, one section climbing a near-vertical cliff by a staircase complete with wooden rungs. But there is a handrail. The Steps route is to be preferred, the cliffs of Wyndcliff offering fine views, while the boulders at their base offer good opportunities for the path to find an adventurous way.

Cross the A466 and continue on the waymarked path through Lower Martridge Wood and into what was once Piercefield Park (see ③ Piercefield Park). When crossing the park the Wye Valley Walk stays among the trees bordering the race course. Pierce Wood is a delightful place, famous in a local story for having been dense enough to disorientate a Chepstow man, who, as dusk arrived, stood in the wood and shouted 'Man lost' with increasing despair. An owl in a nearby tree called 'whooo' and the man yelled 'The Clockmaker from Chepstow' in reply. Or so it said.

A wall in the wood is crossed by stile and soon after a short lane leads to a road. Go left and into Chepstow (see ④ Chepstow). Follow signs and the A48 to Chepstow Castle and cross the Wye beyond using the elegant, but narrow, bridge. At the end of the bridge the main road goes left, but we go ahead up a lane that cuts off the road's sweeping curve up Tutshill. Half-way up this lane the Offa's Dyke Trail joins from the right and we follow its acorn signs to a point just above Tintern. Go over when the main road is regained, leaving the new road on a signed path that reaches the real dyke (see ⑤ Offa's Dyke) before going away from the river to traverse the backs of houses in Woodcroft village to reach Wintour's Leap (see ⑥ Wintour's Leap). Here the path rejoins the road, the B4228, and follows it around a sharp right-hand bend

Tintern Abbey from the Devil's Pulpit

and on for 500m around a left-hand bend. Just after Netherhope Lane has joined the road from the right, having come from Tidenham, a stone stile to the right gives access to a path by a wire fence. Follow this, going over a stile into Wallhope Grove. Follow the right edge of a field, crossing several more stiles to rejoin the B4228. Go right and follow the road for 800m.

As Dennelhill Farm is approached the path goes left, leaving the road to enter the superb woodland of the Wye Valley's eastern bank. The path uses steps to climb up into Boatwood Plantation but thereafter, in Worgan's Wood, the route follows Offa's dyke itself as it contours around the valley side. At Plumweir Cliff the dyke turns sharp right, a turn made to maintain the contour, and continues to the rocky outcrop of the Devil's Pulpit. From here the Devil is said to have preached to the monks building Tintern Abbey, hoping to persuade them to stop their work. About 600m after the Pulpit and Brockweir, we leave the Offa's Dyke Trail, going left on a path, signed for Tintern, that drops down through the woods. Cross a forest track and continue down. Other paths join from the right, but the downhill route is obvious, leading to a cobbled track for a green lane. Go right, crossing the iron bridge over the Wye (see ⑦ Tintern) and going left beyond it to reach the abbey car-park.

① *Tintern Abbey*

Tintern Abbey was one of the high spots of the Wye Tourer's journey, and this is no surprise, the abbey ruins being sufficiently complete to show how the building must have looked and to convey its beauty, and yet being sufficiently ruinous and in such a delightful spot as to be truly romantic. The Revd William

Gilpin, one of the most renowned Tourers, was a leading light of the movement that sought the Picturesque at places like Tintern Abbey. The seekers of the Picturesque roamed the country looking for views, which might even be looked at through a hand-held frame. Gilpin laid down the rules. 'Nature' he said, 'is always great in design ...but she is seldom so correct in composition, as to produce a harmonious whole'. A view, the good reverend gentleman explained, must have an 'area', two 'side-screens' and a 'front-screen'. Any view could, therefore, be marked out of ten for its composition. Low marks, presumably, made Nature blush with embarrassment. Gilpin found the Abbey to be 'an elegant Gothic pile', but though he found parts beautiful, 'the whole is ill-shaped'. He decided that 'a mallet judiciously used (but who durst use it?) might be of service'.

The Abbey was founded in 1131 for Cistercian monks, though what we see today derives almost entirely from a major rebuilding in the 13th century. The cloisters are later, probably from the 15th century. Little is known of the Abbey's history as its records have not come down to us, but it can be assumed that the monks, certainly the early ones, were as industrious as all Cistercians were and had a major impact on the local economy. Henry VIII's Act of Dissolution was applied to Tintern in 1536, and the lead was stripped off the roof to expand the royal coffers. Devoid of their roofs all the dissolved abbeys decayed quickly. At Tintern the Abbey fared better than elsewhere as there were fewer locals to plunder the ruins for building stone. What remains is a magnificent insight into early medieval architecture – the windows are the finest Gothic windows in Britain – and the monastic way of life. Please do take the time to visit.

② Wyndcliff

Wyndcliff is a fine outcrop of limestone set high above the Wye. At its top is a famous viewpoint known as the Eagle's Nest, from which the view is superb, one of the finest in the whole valley. From close to the Eagle's nest the 365 Steps lead to the base of the cliff. They were constructed in 1828 by staff of the Duke of Beaufort after the area had become famous with lovers and other 'romantics' (poets and the like!). The steps were renovated in the early 1970s by apprentices from the Beachley Army College. They did a fine job but reputedly reduced the number of steps to around 300.

③ Piercefield Park

Piercefield Park was once the home of Valentine Morris who laid out a walk with ten viewpoints each supposed to embody the requirements of the Picturesque (see Note ① above). Each viewpoint had a fanciful name – The Chinese Sea, the Grotto, the Druid's Temple – and they were constructed by a Chepstow-based landscape gardener. The layout cost Morris a fortune, the fortune his father had made from Antiguan sugar plantations. Morris's father also left him the plantations, the income from which Morris used to finance a lavish lifestyle. When, in 1770, giant ants ate the cane Morris was bankrupted and had to sell Piercefield to settle his debts. He left Chepstow for Antigua, and as he rode through the town the muffled church bell rang and crowds lined the streets. In the West Indies he revived his fortunes and was appointed Lieutenant General of St Vincent. He lost everything when the French invaded and despite the fact that he had financed a spirited defence from his own pocket, England's ungrateful government imprisoned him for bankruptcy. The injustice was never rectified and Morris died in poverty.

Later, before the race-course took over some of the parkland, the woods were famous for poachers. One was caught and taken to court in Chepstow. His defence was straightforward. 'Indeed your honour I never shot no pheasants at all. The only bird I shot was a rabbit, and I knocked that down with a stick'. Case dismissed surely.

④ *Chepstow*

The old Welsh name for the town was Ystraigyl, *The Bend*, from its position on the Wye. The Normans, when they came, used this name, calling their castle Striguil, *but gradually the Saxon name – meaning market town, the prefix cheap for market also surviving in London's Cheapside and many villages with the word chipping in their name – became the common form.*

The castle dates from the 11th century though most of what we now see is much later. It is a massive fortress, one of the most imposing in Britain, its huge walls sitting right on the Wye's sheer cliff. To add to the impressive nature of the castle the town walls, from the 13th century, are almost complete and have a fine gate, still used to take the traveller into the town. One member of the de Clare family, Norman aristocracy, that held the castle for the king was Gilbert Strongbow, the surname deriving from his extraordinarily long and powerful arms. Gilbert also had five fingers (in addition to the thumb) on each hand, despite all of which he was 'a very perfect gentil knight'.

Gilbert was not at the castle when Edward II was held here before being taken to Berkeley Castle and his death, nor when Edward IV's father-in-law was held before being taken to Kenilworth Castle and execution. Later, during the second Civil War of 1648, there was death at the castle itself. It was held by Sir Nicholas Kemeys for the king. The Parliamentarians stormed the castle after an offer of terms had been refused. Many Royalists were killed, and a plaque marks the spot where Kemeys himself died. Later, with an irony lost on all at the time, the castle was the prison of Sir Henry Marten, one of those who had signed Charles I's death warrant. Marten, imprisoned after the Restoration, was unrepentant until his death. He is buried in the town church.

Visitors used to the Edwardian castles of North Wales will find Chepstow's long, narrow design strange, but there is no doubting the superb engineering of the site, and the views alone make a visit very worthwhile.

⑤ Offa's Dyke

The real reason for the construction of the dyke remains a mystery, the idea that it represents a defensive barrier against the marauding Celts occasionally losing ground in academic arguments to the idea that it was a negotiated political or trade boundary. Either way it was never completed, the final section to Prestatyn in North Wales being abandoned after Offa was killed in a battle with the Celts. Some say that the battle was over the line the final section should take which, if true, casts doubt on the negotiated boundary idea. Along its length the dyke is occasionally difficult to see, but in Worgan's Wood it is very obvious indeed, an eye-catching ridge from a distance, revealed as a huge rampart on closer inspection.

The Offa's Dyke National Trail, a section of which our walk follows, if briefly, starts at Sedbury Cliffs on the Severn's banks near Chepstow and follows the line of the dyke, as far as is possible, all the way to Prestatyn.

⑥ Wintour's Leap

The huge, very steep and somewhat loose, limestone cliffs here are a *favourite with rock climbers. They are named for Sir John Wintour, a Royalist who fortified his Lydney mansion and held it for the king during the Civil War. He was actually away from the house when a Parliamentarian army arrived, but his wife captained the guard on his behalf, and the Cromwellians withdrew, fed up with the struggle. Sir John was not at home because he was attempting to fortify the Severn's banks at Beachley, aware that the river was easily crossed from here to Aust – a fact later used by a river ferry that was made redundant by the first Severn Bridge. As Sir John and his men worked they were surprised by a Parliamentarian force and scrambled down the shallow cliffs to escape. Sir John's feat of scrambling down on horseback gave birth to a local legend that he had leapt these huge cliffs, and the cliffs were named in his honour. One look at the drop will dissuade the walker from the idea that Sir John leapt here.*

⑦ Tintern

Tintern village grew up around the Abbey, there being no authenticated history of occupation of the site before then, though the name derives from the Welsh Din Teyrn, *from* Dinas Teyrn, *the fortress of Teyrn, King of Morgannwg (Glamorgan). The legend has Teyrn being killed at a fortified site here during a battle with Saxon invaders at the end of the 6th century.*

Following the dissolution of the Abbey the village's fortunes declined, but there was a revival in the 17th century when the combination of local supplies of timber for charcoal, iron ore, and the river for transport, gave birth to an iron industry with furnaces beside the river. The local wire works was of great national importance and brass was made here for the first time in Britain. The iron bridge dates from this industrial era, the plate on it recalling that it once carried a tramway to the wire works.

Appendix

WEATHER

A daily forecast, and weather for the next two days, for the Brecon Beacons National Park is posted on the Park's website. The Pembrokeshite Coast National Park website has a link to www.uk.weather.yahoo.com

For more direct information for the Pembrokeshite Park, and other areas of South Wales it is best to telephone:

For the Pembroke and Carmarthen areas – 09014 722064
For the Glamorgan and Monmouth areas – 09014 722059

TRANSPORT

The book covers a large area, and specific information on transport is, consequently, not really possible. For information on your chosen walk area try www.traveline-cymru.org.uk. Transport for the linear Preseli walk is dealt with in the text of that walk.

USEFUL ADDRESSES

Brecon Beacons National Park

Head Office
Plas y Ffynnon
Cambrian Way
Brecon
Powys LD3 7HP
Tel: 01874 624437

Fax: 01874 622574
e-mail:enquiries@breconbeacons.org
The Park's website is www.breconbeacons.org

There are information offices at:

Mountain Centre
Libanus
Brecon
Powys LD3 8ER
Tel: 01874 623366
Fax: 01874 624515
e-mail:mountain.centre@breconbeacons.org

Open: March, April, September, October daily 9.30 – 5; May,
June daily 9.30 – 5.30; July, August daily 9.30 – 5.30;
November – February daily 9.30 – 4.30.

Craig-y-nos Country Park
Pen y Cae
Swansea Valley SA9 1GL
Tel/Fax: 01639 730395
e-mail:cyncp@breconbeacons.org

Open: May Monday – Friday 10.00 – 6.00, Saturday &
Sunday 10.00-7.00
June-August: Monday – Thursday 10.00 – 6.00, Friday –
Sunday 10.00-7.00
September, October, March and April: Monday – Friday 10.00 –
5.00, Saturday & Sunday 10.00 – 6.00
November to February: Monday – Friday 10.00 – 4.00,
Saturday & Sunday 10.00 – 4.30
NOTE: the openings times above are for the Country Park.
Park staff also operate the Visitor Centre and so the Centre
may not be open if Park work requires them to be elsewhere.

Swan Meadow
Monmouth Road
Abergavenny NP7 5E
Tel: 01873 853254

Open: Easter – October daily 10.00 – 1.00, 1.45 – 5.30

The Heritage Centre
Town Centre
Llandovery SA20 0AW
Tel: 01550 720693

Open: Easter-October daily 10.00 – 1.00, 1.45 – 5.30.
October – Easter: Monday – Saturday 10.00-1.00,
1.45 – 400, Sunday 2.00 – 4.00.

There is also a study centre:
Danywenallt Study Centre
Talybont-on-Usk
Brecon
Powys LD3 7YS
Tel: 01874 676677
Fax: 01874 676688
e-mail: danywenallt@breconbeacons.org

Pembrokeshire Coast National Park
Head Office
Llanion Park
Pembroke Dock
Pembrokeshire SA72 6DY
Tel: 0845 345 7275
Fax: 01646 689076
e-mail: info@pembrokeshirecoast.org.uk
The Park's website is: www.pembrokeshirecoast.org

There are Park offices at:

The Grove
St Davids
Haverfordwest
Pembrokeshire SA62 6NW
Tel: 01437 720392
Fax: 01437 720099
e-mail: enquiries@stdavids.pembrokeshirecoast.org.uk

Open: all year except Christmas and early January, Monday –
Saturday 10.00 – 4.00

2 Bank Cottage
Long Street
Newport
Pembrokeshire SA42 0TM
Tel: 01239 820912
e-mail: newportTIC@pembrokeshirecoast.org.uk

Open: all year except Christmas and early January, Monday –
Saturday 10.00 – 4.00

There are also excellent Tourist Information Offices at Cardigan,
Fishguard Haverfordwest, Kilgetty, Milford Haven, Pembroke,
Pembroke Dock, Saundersfoot and Tenby, all of which have
information on not only the local area, but the National Park.

Forest of Dean

The local office of the Forestry Commission is at:

Bank House
Coleford
Gloucestershire GL16 8BA

Tel: 01594 833057
Fax: 01594 833908
e-mail: Dean@forestry.gsi.gov.uk
Website: www.forestry.gov.uk

There is a forest office at:
Beechenhurst Lodge
On the B4226 Coleford to Cinderford road, 500m east of the
junction with the B4234 Lydney to Lydbrook road.
Tel: 01594 827357
Open: daily in Summer 10.00 – 6.00. Every weekend in
winter and some weekdays (same times).

There is also an excellent Tourist Information Office at:
High Street
Coleford
Gloucestershire GL16 8HG
Tel: 01594 812388
Fax: 01594 812330
e-mail: tourism@fdean.gov.uk
website: www.forestofdean.gov.uk

Other Organisations

Cadw
Plas Carew
Unit 5/7Cefn Coed
Parc Nantgarw
Cardiff
CF15 7QQ
Tel: 01443 33 6000
Fax: 01443 33 6001
e-mail: Cadw@Wales.gsi.gov.uk
Website: www.cadw.wales.gov.uk

Countryside Agency
John Dower House
Crescent Place
Cheltenham
Gloucestershire GL50 3RA
Tel: 01242 521381
e-mail: info@countryside.gov.uk
Website: www. countryside.gov.uk

Countryside Council for Wales
Maes-y-Ffynnon
Penrhosgarnedd
Bangor
Gwynedd LL57 2DW
Tel: 08451 306 229
e-mail: enquiries@ccw.gov.uk
website: www.ccw.gov.uk

Forestry Commission
Silvan House
231 Corstorphine Road
Edinburgh
EH12 7AT
Tel: 0131 334 0303 or 0845 FORESTS (0845 3673787)
Fax: 0131 314 6152
e-mail: enquiries@forestry.gsi.gov.uk
website: www. forestry.gsi.gov.uk

National Trust
Head Office
PO Box 39
Warrington WA5 7WD
Tel: 0870 458 4000
Fax: 020 8466 6824

e-mail: enquiries@thenationaltrust.org.uk
website: www.nationaltrust.org.uk

Welsh Office
Trinity Square
Llandudno
LL30 2DE
Tel: 01492 860123
Fax: 01492 860233

Index